# THE BOOK OF HOPE

## OF

## HOPE

### 250 WAYS TO FIND PROMISE AND POSSIBILITY IN SITUATIONS BIG AND SMALL

**CARLEY CENTEN**

Adams Media

New York   London   Toronto   Sydney   New Delhi

Adams Media
An Imprint of Simon & Schuster, Inc.
57 Littlefield Street
Avon, Massachusetts 02322

First Adams Media trade paperback edition January 2021

ADAMS MEDIA and colophon are trademarks of Simon & Schuster.

For information about special discounts for bulk purchases, please contact Simon & Schuster Special Sales at 1-866-506-1949 or business@simonandschuster.com.

The Simon & Schuster Speakers Bureau can bring authors to your live event. For more information or to book an event contact the Simon & Schuster Speakers Bureau at 1-866-248-3049 or visit our website at www.simonspeakers.com.

Interior image © 123RF/elenarolau

Manufactured in the United States of America

10 9 8 7 6 5 4 3 2 1

Library of Congress Cataloging-in-Publication Data has been applied for.

ISBN 978-1-5072-1538-8
ISBN 978-1-5072-1539-5 (ebook)

# Introduction

Hope is more than a fleeting feeling—it's a way of seeing the inherent change and uncertainty of life as full of potential, mystery, and grounded action. It's what we draw on when things seem bleak. But it's also the fuel with which we can charge at life with optimism and resilience. Though it's not always easy to remain hopeful through loss, difficulty, and the everyday challenges of life, *The Book of Hope* provides what you need to restore your sense of possibility, whatever life throws your way.

Throughout the book, you'll find 250 unique ways to fill yourself with trust, confidence, and hope, including:

- Mindfulness exercises
- Thought experiments
- Inspirational quotes
- Body and breathwork
- Writing and journaling prompts
- Creative ideas
- And more…

From planting a seed to changing your thought patterns and building emotional regulation, the ideas in this book will give you skills and ways to be hopeful, whether you're just trying to get through the day—or working toward building your best life.

If you need a port in the storm as well as an outlook that will take you from surviving to thriving, this book is for you. *The Book of Hope* has just what you need to heal, inspire, and build yourself up—anytime you need it.

✦

This awful catastrophe is not the end but the beginning. History does not end so. It is the way its chapters open.

—SAINT AUGUSTINE
*Roman-African theologian and philosopher*

# Set an Affirmation for Hope

What do you hope for? It can be tempting to place your hopes in something specific. A fancy car. A dream job. A perfect relationship. See what it feels like to release your expectation of a specific outcome. At its most basic, hope is your aspiration to be your best self.

Set a course for your hope with an affirmation. Affirmations are phrases you can repeat to yourself that help to focus you on something you want to internalize and believe in. Set a hopeful affirmation for how you want to be toward yourself, to others, and in your life. For example:

- I am authentic, open, and honest with myself.
- I am kind, compassionate, and understanding with others.
- I am optimistic. I choose hope.

Tailor these affirmations to what you want to cultivate within yourself for a hopeful outlook in your relationship with yourself and others, and in your experiences. Close your eyes and repeat them to yourself every day when you first wake up to set the tone for your day.

# Light a Candle

A common metaphor for hope is that it is like a light in the dark. When your hopes are dashed and you don't know where to go from here, it can feel like fumbling around in a cave without a flashlight. It's scary and paralyzing. But you can bring the light, as if you're turning on a switch, and step out of the shadows. Light a candle as a literal interpretation of this idea and as a reminder that within the darkness, hope can light the way.

1. Block out the light in a room. This might be best done at night to make it easier to do so.
2. Strike a match and light a single candle.
3. Watch the flame with a relaxed gaze and bring your awareness to your breath. Notice any scent you can smell. It might be a fragranced candle or it might be the lingering smell of the match or the fire itself.
4. With every in-breath that you take, draw in the light, imagining it flooding your body with warmth, moving in you with every breath.
5. With every out-breath, breathe out the darkness. Let go of tension and any tightness in your body.
6. Repeat these breaths for a few minutes, watching the flickering flame, noticing how the light spreads outward into the darkness, and noticing how you feel as you invite the light within yourself.

# Name What You Feel

When you're despairing and trying to reach for hope, you might feel anything but. Emotions can seem big and overwhelming. This exercise seems simple, but being able to regulate how you feel is a master skill that unlocks huge potential in your ability to weather the storms of life and keep your course set on hope. Examine what you're feeling through the following four steps of "R.A.I.N."

1. **R**ecognize the emotion. Put a label on it and a specific name to it.
2. **A**cknowledge the feeling. Allow it to be as it is. You might be used to pushing away negative feelings. What would it be like to let it be here for now?
3. **I**nvestigate the feeling in your body. Does it show up in how you hold yourself? Does it cause any tension or strain or stress within you when you really focus on this feeling?
4. **N**urture the feeling. This means that you recognize it is with you now, but you are not this feeling. You don't need to overly identify with it as something that says something about you as a person or your situation.

Notice how you feel now. What are the contours of the edges of the feeling? It might be subtle, but you may notice the power of the emotion shift or other feelings entering the picture. Make room for them as they are, name them, and see if this process can help you allow them to dissolve.

✦

# Hope is the belief that destiny will not be written for us, but by us.

—BARACK OBAMA
*Forty-fourth president of the United States*

# Craft Your Mission Statement

Hope can feel like an abstract wish for things to be better than they are. A positive dream for yourself is important, but just as important is having an idea of where you want to direct these intentions. If it's unclear to you now, try this exercise to create a mission statement for yourself. A mission statement gets into the heart of what motivates you and why you do what you do. It's like a North Star you can come back to, to guide you whenever you need a reminder of what it's all for.

Complete the following sentence by answering the questions in the brackets:

*I [what do you do?—think actions and verbs] so that [why do you do it?].*

This sentence can help show you the contributions that you make. It's more than just a quality or virtue you want to cultivate within yourself. Perhaps your quality is that you're a good friend. Make it your mission to check in on how your friends are so that they know they are cared for. Spend some time thinking about the most important things you feel you do, who you do those things for, and what they're for. Come back to this statement any time you need a reminder to stay on course.

# Take Stock

When it feels as though everything in your life is going wrong, you might lose all hope. The truth is, it's rare that a difficulty or problem truly affects every aspect of your life. It might only feel like what you face is all-pervasive because it looms large in front of you as an all-consuming loss, change, or setback. Take stock of all aspects of your life to gain some perspective by drawing a Wheel of Life.

1. Draw a large circle on a piece of paper and divide it into eight pieces like a pizza.
2. Label each segment with the following categories: Health, Friends and Family, Significant Other, Personal Growth, Fun and Leisure, Home Environment, Career, and Money.
3. Imagine that the outer edge of the circle represents being perfectly satisfied with that aspect of your life and is a ten out of ten. The center point of the circle is a zero, representing completely unsatisfied. In each of the eight categories, draw a dot representing how close to zero or ten you feel that aspect of your life is right now. Don't overthink it—go with where your gut says you feel you are.
4. Connect the dots from one segment to the next, drawing a web within your larger circle.
5. Reflect on where your lines are unbalanced or closer to zero. This gives you a visual of where things are going well, for which you can be grateful, and which aspects of your life need care right now.

# Consider *Memento Mori*

It might sound a bit morbid to think about an old phrase from Latin, *memento mori*, which means "Remember, you must die." Death doesn't usually sound like a particularly hopeful topic. Consider, however, that there are few things certain in life, but the fact that every human will one day close their eyes for the last time is one of them. Reflecting on this fact can be motivating rather than defeating. If you remember that time is precious, you focus more on what matters and the quality of life you want to live while you can. It can make you cherish what you have now, rather than waiting to live when things are somehow "better," different, or as you'd hope for them to be in the future. Ask yourself the following questions:

- If today were your last day on Earth, would you want to spend it doing what you are doing? If your answer is "no," how many of these kinds of days are making up your life right now?
- If you knew you had one year left to live, how would you spend it? Are there differences between what you would do and how you're living now? Is there a way you could close that gap?

Of course there are days you need to do things you'd rather not and times you need to sacrifice in order to obtain something worthwhile later. But it's worth considering whether you're making the best use of the limited time you have to truly live.

◆

When trust is shattered, when hopes are dashed, when a loved one leaves you, before doing anything, just pause your life and rest a moment.

—HAEMIN SUNIM
*South Korean teacher and Buddhist writer*

# Pause and Ground Yourself

It can be difficult to maintain your positivity when you're over-whelmed. You might be triggered by something that causes you to spiral, shut down, or dissociate. Or, you might be pulled under by hard-to-handle emotions. This little sensing exercise is good for halting the descent of intrusive thoughts and will help ground yourself in the present. It's one that you can remember and access wherever you are, whenever you feel overwhelmed.

1. When you catch your thoughts or emotions getting out of your control, pause what you're doing.
2. Looking around where you are, name five things you can see.
3. Name four things you can feel. It might be clothing against your skin, a breeze on your face, or your fingertips holding something.
4. Name three things you can hear, far or near.
5. Name two things you can smell.
6. Name one thing you can taste.
7. Notice at the end of this exercise how you feel and whether you feel more in control.

# Start a Mindful Meditation Practice

Mindfulness is more than just a buzzword or an app—it's another master skill that enables you to positively work with your mind and body. By developing a greater awareness of your thought patterns, your emotions, and your experiences through a meditation practice, you can be less reactive in your day-to-day life and develop greater resilience. Learn to catch the patterns that lead you to feeling hopeless and reorient yourself to hope.

1. Find a quiet place where you can sit comfortably and won't be interrupted.
2. Set a timer for ten to fifteen minutes.
3. Close your eyes or rest your gaze, taking your attention to your breath, noticing every inhale and every exhale through your nose.
4. Any time your mind wanders from this focus on your breath, notice it by saying "thinking" to yourself and guide your attention back to your breath. Know that it's completely normal for your mind to wander and not a sign that you're doing it "wrong." The main thing is to try not to resist the thoughts that come or push them away because this can make the thought even stickier in your mind. It might help to notice if your thought is about the past or future as you acknowledge it and return your focus to your breath.
5. When the timer goes, slowly blink your eyes open. Notice how you feel.

# Grieve Your Losses

It might surprise you to read this heading in a book about hope. Grief is associated with sadness, pain, and loss. But it's often during these experiences and feelings that we most need to find our way back to a sense of hope. This exercise isn't one you can just do and be done. The truth is, the only way out is through. Allow yourself the space and time to feel everything you feel. Some things in life can't be fought through with brute force, they must be felt and carried. Grief can have its stages, but it is often not a linear process. It is okay to step forward and backward through this. Great loss is a measure of great feeling. It is a testament to your care, the depth of your offering, and your precious vulnerability. Make space to feel it and find comfort where you can too. Take your hand to your heart. Feel your heartbeat in the here and now. Cherish this beat.

✦

What kept me
sane was knowing
that things would
change, and it was a
question of keeping
myself together
until they did.

—NINA SIMONE
*American singer-songwriter and activist*

# Simply Stop

To hold on to hope doesn't mean you need to grasp and cling to it tightly, as if you were to look away it would disappear. Instead, relax into it. Let it soften you, rather than create hard edges. When you notice yourself feeling desperation rather than hope, take this "stop" break developed by psychologists to help you build emotional resilience in the moment.

1. Stop whatever you're doing and pause.
2. Take a breath and bring your awareness to your inhales and exhales.
3. Observe your mind. What were you just thinking about?
4. Pull back for some perspective. Zoom out. Where does this fit into your wider life? What aspects of your life does it touch? What aspects does it not touch? How important is this right now? Where are you clinging to a specific expectation or outcome?
5. Proceed. Move on to something that works for you. What action do you want to take right now? Perhaps it's to reorient to something else. Perhaps it's to take action on whatever has come up. Perhaps it's to soften and relax and let go. Take your next best action.

# Reset to What's Important

When you're in the midst of the storm, when things are difficult, exhausting, or painful, you might be in a kind of day-to-day survival mode. These are times when it's especially difficult to be hopeful about the future. During these times you might need to reset your expectations and come back to the things that are most important to your well-being.

Write down five things that are important for you to do every day. Stick the list on a Post-it note at your desk or put it somewhere you will see it, like your fridge or bathroom mirror.

Think of small, regular little habits that make you feel good. Set aside any impulse to think you "should" be doing more or setting big, hairy goals. This is about making things easier on you, not harder—to give yourself the care you need to keep going. Perhaps you want to take five minutes to sit quietly with your coffee in the morning. Perhaps it's a bit of time to stretch or meditate or talk to a friend. It can be as simple as drinking water throughout the day or journaling.

Commit to doing these five small things every day for the next week. At the end of the week, check in with yourself. Are these habits starting to more easily become part of your day? Are they helping you to feel more empowered to keep going through this time of survival?

# Ask for Help

You might try to dig deep within yourself to find hope, but hope can also be a collective experience. When your cup is empty, lower it into the well to draw on strength from others. Find hope in others and build hope together. You don't have to bear everything alone, like a great weight you carry on your shoulders. Ask for help. It's not a weakness; it's actually a sign of true strength. You are strong when you are capable of doing things for yourself. You're even stronger when you can allow someone else to do something for you. It's a strength founded in vulnerability—in taking the risk to open yourself up to what someone else has to offer and give. If you're not used to asking for help, think of something small that someone could easily assist you with, and identify someone you trust in your life who would be in a good position to do so. Reach out and practice asking for help.

✦

I've found that
there is always
some beauty left—
in nature, sunshine,
freedom, in
yourself; these can
all help you.

—ANNE FRANK
*German-Dutch diarist*

# Don't Make It Personal

Dr. Martin Seligman identified some sticky beliefs that block your ability to be optimistic and resilient. One such belief is that what you face is personal—that whatever has happened is your fault. You might blame yourself for everything and launch into projects to try to prevent anything like this from happening again. You might feel you need a form of closure. There's a natural belief that if you could only understand things better, do things better, *be* better, then you could do everything right and prevent bad things from happening. But the truth is, adversity is simply a part of life. Often it's not personal, and the influence you have over things is smaller than you'd think. Understand that much of what happens to you is not personal. You can't foresee every possible negative outcome and prevent it. What's more, blaming yourself doesn't help you move forward. Instead, see how it feels to accept things as they are with this mantra: "I forgive myself."

# Get Back Up

The feeling that whatever you're dealing with is all-pervasive is another resilience-blocking belief. The idea that the hardship you're facing affects every facet of your life is often false. Some of the greatest struggles you'll face will in fact impact more than one aspect of your life, but it's rare that all is lost. Consider the most stable things in your life—where you live, what you do, and who you spend time with. When you experience great change or instability in one of these areas, it can rock your world. When more than one area is affected, the stress is magnified. It can feel like an earthquake has hit and disrupted everything. But take stock for a moment of what is still standing. Take note of which aspects of your life you can rely on and feel safe and supported in. Let these be like pillars holding you up while you heal, focusing on this mantra: "I'm still standing."

# Trust In Impermanence

Permanence is an enemy of resilience. If you have an unrealistic belief that what you're dealing with will last forever it can lead to a mindset of resignation. It might be that you need to adjust to a new normal. But nothing is permanent. Even if all that shifts is your attitude, or the way you feel about what has changed for you, trust that it will change. Dismantle any thoughts of permanence with a sense of potential. Think about what you want for yourself in the future. There are times it does feel like nothing will ever be the same. Great losses, great accidents, and great changes can alter your sense of reality, your ideas for the future, and what you believe in. But you will continue to grow, to adapt, to change, to heal. You don't need to know what it will look like yet. Let it be enough for now to know that nothing is forever with this mantra: "This too shall pass."

✦

You can cut all the
flowers but you
cannot keep spring
from coming.

—PABLO NERUDA
*Chilean diplomat and poet*

# Breathe Softly

In the moment, when hope seems lost and you can't see a way out, tapping into the power of your breath is one of the fastest ways you can return to a sense of calm that will ground you. Try this exercise when things are overwhelming you.

1. Sit in a comfortable way so that you can feel relaxed.
2. Take your hands to your belly.
3. Breathe in and say to yourself, "soft," letting your belly move without trying to hold it in or restrict it in any way. Notice any tendency to suck your belly in or bring tension into your body. Use this reminder to soften and allow your ribs to expand naturally.
4. Breathe out and say to yourself, "belly," keeping your awareness with the movement of the breath in your body and again letting everything relax and empty.
5. Continue breathing in this way with this focus for at least ten breath cycles.
6. Notice how you feel afterward. Can you hold on to this feeling of softness throughout your being?

# Find Good Luck

The phrase "with my luck" usually has a negative meaning. But this is only because it depends on what you pay attention to. There's a natural tendency to remember the negative things and to think you have all the bad luck. But it's more likely that you are simply not paying as close attention to the good luck.

Why not make "with my luck" a positive phrase that attunes you to all the good things? With my luck, things will go even better than I imagined. With my luck, I'll find exactly what I need. With my luck, I'll get there even faster than I planned.

Another way to look at luck is simply as a story that is still in the middle rather than the end. The farmer with the lost horse is a good example. Everyone pitied the farmer's bad luck, but he shrugged: "Good luck, bad luck, who knows?" The horse returned later with a whole herd of wild horses. The tale continues to recount things that seem like tragedies at the time, but later turn out to be blessings.

Think about the last time something happened to you that made you feel you were struck by bad luck. What did you do? What did you learn? How did it change you? What did it bring into your life that otherwise wouldn't have happened?

# Be Mindful of Unhelpful Thoughts

If you are discouraged and despondent, it might help to realize that you are not your thoughts. It seems a strange concept at first. You have within you a thinking mind, running like trains on a track, crafting stories all day long. But you also have an observing mind that can step back with openness and curiosity to watch this show unfold with more objectivity. With mindfulness, you can practice separating your thinking mind from your observing mind, which can help you to sort through which thoughts you want to pay attention to.

When you find yourself being carried away by the stories your narrating mind is creating, pause to examine these thoughts. If they're negative and bothering you, resist the urge to push them away or force yourself to stop thinking about them. Instead, notice the quality of the thoughts you are having. If it is causing you to worry, fear, and despair and isn't useful in helping you deal with the root of these anxieties, tell your narrating mind: "unhelpful." Notice if acknowledging this thought and labeling it this way allows you to surrender the narration and refocus on what better serves you.

◆

Some of us think holding on makes us strong but sometimes it is letting go.

—HERMANN HESSE
*German-Swiss writer and painter*

# Talk about the Highlights— and Lowlights

You're primed to notice the negative things so that you'll take action. But this can mean you more easily recall the bad stuff and might imagine that these difficulties will last longer than they are likely to. When this happens, it might cloud your hopes for the future because all you can see are the things that are going wrong and it can feel like it will always be like this. It's important to take the time on a regular basis to acknowledge what's going well. Generate a more balanced view by reflecting daily on the highlights and lowlights of the day.

This is a great one you can do at the dinner table with friends and family or before bed with kids or partners as you say goodnight. Reflecting on the day you've just had, what was the best thing that happened? What was the worst thing that happened? Share these with each other or write them down in a journal. Reflect on what these highlights and lowlights tell you about your life and what is important to you.

# Take the Opposite Action

It's not pleasant feeling frustrated. You feel like things are not going your way and you're unable to influence the situation, which is a death knell to hope. Reactions to frustration often don't help. Perhaps you shut down or avoid things. Maybe you get into arguments or disengage with the silent treatment. These are protest behaviors that could temporarily make you feel you have a small bit of control, but they don't get to the root of the issue or create any change in what you're dealing with. Often, these strategies make things even worse.

Try this thought experiment. When you're annoyed, angry, or upset, tackle these emotions by doing the opposite of what your usual impulse is. Rather than acting based on what you feel, do the opposite and see how what you feel changes. Instead of shutting down, get up and move your body. Instead of fighting with the source of your frustration, accept it. Instead of raising your voice and making fists, speak quietly and relax your body.

Can you think of the opposite of what you want to do now? Do that thing! Notice if it interrupts your usual way of reacting to frustrating emotions and guides you to a more productive way forward.

✦

Sometimes we have to do the work even though we don't yet see a glimmer on the horizon that it's actually going to be possible.

—ANGELA DAVIS
*American activist and author*

# Draw a Picture Without Looking

When you're fixated on an outcome, your sense of hope is rigid. If you base your hopes in expectations, you set yourself up for disappointment. Let your hopes guide how they will be fulfilled. Try this creative drawing exercise to practice letting go of a focus on the outcome and enjoy the process itself.

1. Set a timer for five minutes.
2. Draw your hand on a sheet of paper with a pencil or pen. Here's the catch: You're not allowed to look at your paper or the hand that holds the pencil and does the drawing.
3. Look at your subject hand and capture as much detail as you can. The individual fingers, knuckles, lines, and wrinkles. Drawing hands is difficult even for trained artists, so let go and see what you can do!
4. When the timer ends, look at what you've created. It's unlikely to look much like a hand at all. It might be abstract and beautiful in its own way. Reflect on how you felt in this process, where you do not have to worry about the picture you make, but are free to let the pen move and create what it will.

# Become Your Alter Ego

If you doubt yourself and what your capabilities are, you'll struggle to embody a sense of potential and hope within yourself. This can lead to inaction and spiraling self-doubt as you "prove" your fears correct. When you feel ill-equipped, try pretending you're someone else. It's a technique that coaches use with top athletes to improve their performance beyond the limits they set for themselves. And it's something great thinkers and artists use to insert some distance between the doubting chatter in their mind and what it is they're trying to achieve.

Think of someone you admire who has done what you're trying to do. Perhaps it's a favorite writer, athlete, or actor. It could be someone you know who has faced something similar to what you're facing now. Imagine the qualities you think they must have that make them good at what they do. Imagine for a moment that you are them. Take on their name. Take on those qualities. Wherever you are, embody their confidence, holding your head high and lengthening your posture. Keep yourself in this alter ego state as you start to tackle what you need to. Notice how you feel.

# Record Your Gratitude

It might just be impossible to feel sorry for yourself if you're busy feeling thankful instead. Try this journaling exercise to banish self-pity with positivity.

Every night before you go to bed, write down three things you were most grateful for that day. Focus on experiences that made you feel something. Make them specific rather than vague. They don't have to be grand events. In fact, this is about noticing the everyday things. The feel of the breeze on your face. The taste of your morning coffee. The laughter of a friend. The way your dog greeted you. A slice of dessert.

It is important to do this journaling technique consistently. It's actually less about keeping a record of what you're grateful for and more about how this practice habituates you to noticing the good things in your daily life. You might find yourself recognizing the moments as they come up, wondering, will this be my most grateful moment today? Or is the best still to come? This way of seeing positions you to be more aware of what lights you up and what you want to bring more of into your life.

✦

# In the midst of winter, I found there was, within me, an invincible summer.

—ALBERT CAMUS
*French philosopher and author*

# Love Yourself

A big barrier to showing up for yourself with optimism and hope is whether you truly feel you deserve good things. When was the last time you really held yourself in unconditional love? Do you carry feelings of self-aversion and unworthiness within you that you avoid confronting? Take some time to nurture your relationship with yourself the way you would any of your deepest relationships with others with this little meditation of self-love. Try this practice every day for a week and notice if how you feel toward yourself shifts, allowing you to let more love in.

1. Set a timer for five minutes and sit comfortably somewhere quiet.
2. Take your focus to your breath, noticing the feel and temperature of the air and where the breath moves in your body.
3. With every inhale, say to yourself: "I love myself."
4. Notice how you feel as you say these words to yourself. Do you believe it? Or are there parts of you resisting this feeling? Is there tension in your mind and body?
5. With every exhale, let go of any resistance. Relax any tension you hold in your body, from your jaw to your shoulders to your hips.
6. Keep breathing with this focus until your timer goes, inhaling love in, exhaling any barriers within you to accepting this love from yourself.

# Laugh It Up

Optimists can seem like a funny bunch—literally. People who see the glass as half full use humor in a way that diffuses other intense emotions. When you're feeling low, find something that makes you laugh, whether it's a favorite comedian, or a friend you can count on for a wisecrack or silly meme. You can also just start laughing without any stimulus. It feels weird at first, but this laughter meditation can actually give you similar benefits, producing a greater sense of control when things are overwhelming. Here's how to try it.

You can do this on your own, but if you're with a friend or group, lie down with your head resting on a friend's belly, arranging yourselves so that everyone is cuddled up with someone else in this way.

1. With your awareness on your breath, take a big yawn, inhaling through your mouth. As you exhale, sigh it out with an audible and satisfying sound.
2. Smile softly to yourself.
3. Start to widen your smile, baring your teeth and crinkling your eyes, pushing up your cheeks.
4. Start to chuckle and laugh.
5. Shake your whole body into raucous laughter. If you're in a group, someone's laugh will inevitably really get you going and set off a chain reaction that percolates throughout the group through both the sound and the physical shakes of laughter taking over.
6. Notice how you feel afterward and if there is more lightness to what was heavy at the start.

# Take a Hero's Journey

The Hero's Journey is a common plot in epics and stories. The hero usually starts in the ordinary world as it is, but then they receive the call for adventure. At first, they refuse this call because it represents the unknown and they are afraid. But a mentor appears who provides wisdom and guidance. The would-be hero crosses over into the unknown world, where they are tested and need to break through their fears. They encounter difficulties and crises through which they might land at rock bottom. This is a kind of symbolic death—a letting go of everything they thought they knew in the real world. But they rise from these ashes, reborn. When they overcome all of the challenges set out for them, and especially when they change on the inside, they are able to return to the real world, but they are forever changed. They can even share what they've learned to help others so that the problems or mistakes of the past aren't repeated.

It's a powerful metaphor of personal transformation and the journey you might take when you start to question what you think you know to realize your hopeful future. You might resist change you know you need to go through. You might refuse and fight until it becomes more uncomfortable to keep struggling against it than to move into it and let it change you. Take some time to think about where you are on this journey, where you are refusing the call, where you are being challenged, and where you will come out reborn.

◆

This is a good sign, having a broken heart. It means we have tried for something.

—ELIZABETH GILBERT
*American author*

# Create a Circle of Compassion

Hope isn't something you only hold for yourself; hope is important for communities and can be both strongest and most needed as a shared wish for better things. For people to take more care of each other. For people to feel connected rather than isolated. For real change to take hold in people's lives. Develop collective hope through compassion. This is the focus of a Buddhist meditation called *tonglen*, which means "sending and taking." It's a generous act of witnessing the suffering of others and responding with ease and relaxation.

1. Sit in a way that is most comfortable for you.
2. Bring your focus to your breath, breathing through your nose.
3. Relax your gaze in front of you or close your eyes.
4. With every inhale, draw in the suffering of others.
5. With every exhale, breathe out healing, peace, and hope.
6. Continue to breathe in this way for several rounds, taking in what's difficult and painful and sending out compassion.
7. Notice how you feel and whether there is more connection and less distance between you and everything and everyone.

# Take a Soothing Shower

Water is essential to life. More than half of your body is made up of water and you need it for your very survival. This might be why, in evolutionary terms, finding a water source was like finding life. It's an element that is the very embodiment of relief and hope. Tap into this symbolically by taking a soothing shower. In your day-to-day life, you might not take the time to relish in the ritual of bathing. Light a candle in your bathroom, turn out the lights, and treat yourself to a serene moment to yourself. Allow your eyes to relax in the dim flickering light. Try standing with your chin slightly tucked so that the spray finds the crown of your head and waterdrops roll down you like a waterfall enveloping you. Tune in to the sound of the water and meditate on its life-giving rhythm as your focal point. Notice how you feel afterward as you softly pat yourself dry.

# Develop Body Awareness with Yin Yoga

Hope is not only located in your thoughts and feelings. The mind and body are connected. To work with one, you must work with the other, but often it's the mind that takes priority. Alongside mindfulness skills and emotional regulation, body awareness is essential to self-awareness, healing, and resilience. Learn to start listening to your body. Try this twisting exercise from yin yoga—a practice where poses are held for a long time, but not at full intensity.

1. Lie down on your back on a mat or somewhere firm but comfortable.
2. Scan your body from your toes to the top of your head, noticing any internal sensations and how you feel.
3. Take your knees into your chest. Hug them in toward your belly.
4. Keeping your legs bent, release your arms out into a T-shape with your palms down to the ground.
5. Drop your knees to one side. Try this with a pillow to catch your knees in order to lessen the intensity of the twist. You can also put a pillow between your knees if that feels good.
6. Turn your head away from your dropped knees if that's comfortable for you. Again, the goal isn't to experience a full-intensity stretch, but to find a space you can relax into this shape.
7. Stay here for three to five minutes.
8. Unravel back to center and stretch fully with your arms overhead. Notice how one side of your body feels compared to the other.
9. Repeat, dropping your knees to the other side. Again, notice how your entire body feels now.

◆

I learned that
when life pulls you
under, you can kick
against the bottom,
break the surface,
and breathe again.

—SHERYL SANDBERG
*American philanthropist and COO of Facebook*

# Exhale to Calm Anxiety

In a way, you could consider anxiety as rooted in a crisis of hope. It's a fear of things not being okay or thinking that they're not going to be okay. But it's also a natural, evolved process. Your nervous system reacts to stress in order to give your body oxygen and resources to tackle it. The problem comes when you live in this space that was meant to be a temporary boost. This practice uses your ability to control your breath to help find calm.

1. From a comfortable position, notice your natural breath. Notice especially if your usual tendency is to breathe mostly into your chest as opposed to your belly—this can be a sign of anxious breathing.
2. Take a deep cleansing breath in and out through your nose, counting to four for the inhale and to four for the exhale.
3. Next, breathe in to a count of four, but exhale to a count of five.
4. If that's comfortable for you, and you don't find yourself gasping or struggling for air, breathe in for a count of four and out for a count of six.
5. Increase the count on your exhales to seven and then to eight, again, only if this is comfortable.
6. Working at whichever level is suitable for you, take at least five full rounds of breath with these extended exhales. When anxiety is pressing on the gas pedal, longer exhales work almost like a hack to put on the brakes.
7. Let your breath return to its natural rhythm. Notice how you feel.

# Stand in Hope

When you feel physically rundown, your resilience will suffer. In fact, it might be that feeling unwell, tired, or achy is a sign that you're heading for burnout. It's like trying to stand up in quicksand where every step only takes you deeper and there's nothing solid to reach for. Don't ignore what your body is telling you. Slow down. Listen. This simple exercise might help get you out of your head and take time to feel into your body.

1. Stand tall with your feet planted hip-distance apart. Find length throughout your spine, holding your head high with your chin parallel to the ground. Draw your shoulders down away from your ears. Relax your arms by your sides.
2. Take a slow deep breath, noticing where the breath moves in your body.
3. Rock your weight slightly, front to back and side to side on your feet without letting any part of them come off the ground.
4. When you've explored this shift in weight, find a center point where you feel balanced.
5. Next, pick up your toes and wiggle them a bit, taking them up and down off the ground while you keep your heels and the front part of your foot firmly down.
6. Pick up all ten toes and see if you can place them down to the ground one at a time, starting with your littlest toe. This will help to spread your toes, giving you a wider base to stand on.
7. Notice how you feel here from the ground up: physically supported and strong in your body.

# Trust You Can Handle It

If you don't believe in yourself, any hope you have will be flimsy. You might say you want something better, but it's as if you've built your house on sand. It's a kind of hope more characteristic of desperation rather than positive belief. It's important that you truly believe you are capable of facing the challenges you meet in life. If you give in and give up, you are not acting in hope.

Think of a time when you felt out of your depth or unable to handle things. What did you do then? How did you come through it? How did this experience challenge and expand you? Tackle self-doubt with this mantra: "I have handled things before, and I'll handle them again." Remember this phrase and repeat it to yourself whenever you are overwhelmed by what you're facing and need a reminder to trust in yourself.

◆

# The world breaks everyone and afterward many are strong at the broken places.

—ERNEST HEMINGWAY
*American journalist and novelist*

# Become a Warrior

There's a bit of a paradox when it comes to hope. Hope requires a belief that you can influence things in the course of your life. And at the same time, it requires releasing your grip on what is outside of your control! Both skills need to be cultivated and balanced so you can draw on them when you need them. This yoga shape, called Warrior Two, is a powerful stance that can help build the first skill, a sense of being in control of yourself.

1. Stand tall with your feet hip-distance apart.
2. Step one foot backward to come into a lunge with your front knee bent about 90 degrees. This takes a bit of faith in yourself to step back without looking. You can also adjust the width of your stance as needed. Your back heel will be raised.
3. When you've found your footing, turn on your back toes to place your heel down, moving your hips from being forward-facing to opening out to the side. Place your back foot flat, perpendicular to your front foot, which will still be facing straight ahead. Press your weight along the back edge of your back foot. Your front knee is still bent and facing forward, and your back leg is straight and strong.
4. Take your arms out into a T-shape.
5. Count five breaths here, feeling strong and stable.
6. Repeat on the other side and notice how you feel.

# Put Yourself First

Being generous and giving is a beautiful quality. But if you're always self-sacrificing, you will shrink yourself over time. Your hopes will become secondary. You'll learn to be comfortable supporting the dreams of others and not investing in your own. At the root of this thinking could be fear and unworthiness. You might believe you are only worthy and good while you're being useful to others. It's important to put yourself first from time to time. It's not selfish—it's actually going to put you in a better position to give to others. You cannot give from an empty cup, and if you are always self-sacrificing, your cup *will* be emptied. Consider the instruction on a flight to put your own oxygen mask on first in an emergency before helping others. It goes against your instinct—you want to help the person next to you, your family, your children, before yourself. But if you don't put your own mask on first, you'll run out of air and be unable to help anyone.

Identify where you are sacrificing yourself and your needs. Where are you giving out of fear that you need to earn the care and support of others? Where are you giving from a position of strength?

# Tell Your Story

What happens to you isn't just about events. It's also the story you tell around those events. It can be especially difficult to come to terms with traumas and with painful or fragmented memories. Telling a coherent story is a way of taking back control—the kind of control that's important for resilience. Owning your story can help you find a better way forward. It takes you out of unhelpful (though understandable!) ways of relating to your own story such as denial, repression, and dissociation and helps you find safety. Everyone has a story to tell, and every story is valid and important. Try these prompts to start writing or reconstructing yours.

- Write about a time you felt out of place or really uncomfortable.
- Write about something traumatic that happened to you in the third person, as if it happened to someone else.
- Write about a time you experienced big emotions.
- Write about what you learned from a painful experience—the good and the bad.

Try these exercises over the course of a few days and notice if how you feel about your experiences, or the hold they have over you, shifts in any way.

✦

It is the nature of the strong heart, that like the palm tree it strives ever upwards when it is most burdened.

—SIR PHILIP SIDNEY
*English poet, scholar, and soldier*

# Self-Soothe Through Self-Massage

Touch is perhaps your most sensitive sense. When things seem bleak, physical sensations can bring calm to your mind and body. Give yourself a relaxing shoulder and neck massage to tap into the power of touch when you need a boost.

1. Sit comfortably and take some slow, deep breaths.
2. Move your fingers to the side of your neck below your ears. With a light pressure, slide your fingers down toward your shoulders. You can try this with your knuckles as well to find a sensation or pressure that feels good to you. Move very slow—slower than you think you need to—and repeat this motion for several rounds.
3. Take your right hand over your left shoulder. Give your shoulder a squeeze and draw circles on the back of your shoulder with your fingers. Try this while lifting your shoulder up and down or in circles, noticing how this changes the feel of your massage under your fingertips. Repeat this with your left hand over your right shoulder.
4. Finally, place both hands on your shoulders beside the base of your neck. Squeeze your shoulders in your hands and gently pull your fingers from the back of your shoulders forward.
5. Notice how you feel after taking these few moments to slowly, and with care, bring yourself some comfort through massage.

# Visit Your Feelings

In the same way that you are not your thoughts, you are not your feelings either. You could be used to thinking about every feeling as part of you. But think about what you feel as information or as a visitor trying to tell you something. This can help to take the intensity out of what you feel so that you can make room for positivity even when things feel anything but. Here's how to try it.

1. When a large emotion arrives, notice it. Name what you feel as specifically as you can and say it out loud to yourself. For example: "I am sad." "I am angry." "I am hopeless."
2. Take whatever you've identified and rephrase it as a more temporary experience rather than something you *are*. For example: "I am feeling sad." "A part of me is angry." "Sometimes things seem hopeless." Repeat this new formulation out loud to yourself.
3. Notice if this helps to take the power out of the feeling ever so slightly, allowing you to work with whatever arises as an impermanent and not all-consuming visitor.

# Fold Forward

This is one of the simplest ways that you can bring calm to your mind and body when your thoughts are giving way to despair and anxiety. There are many options here from yoga that help put the rest-and-digest side of your nervous system in control. Find one that feels best to you, where you can melt and relax as you bring your belly to rest on your thighs. Spend at least five rounds of breath in any of these folds and notice how you feel.

1.  From sitting in a chair, fold forward from your hips to take your torso over your legs. Let your arms hang down heavy.
2.  From standing, hinge at your waist and fold forward, keeping your legs either straight or bending at your knees slightly. You could clasp your elbows with your opposite hands or bend your knees generously to rest your belly on the tops of your legs. Let your head hang heavy. Don't worry about stretching or how close you come to your legs—this is about letting go.
3.  Sitting on the floor with the soles of your feet planted on the ground and knees bent, hug your legs by wrapping your arms around the back of your thighs. Rest your forehead on top of your knees as you curl your spine.
4.  Take a Child's Pose, sitting back on your heels, either with your knees wide and toes touching, or legs together. Crawl yourself forward, taking your arms out in front of you or resting them by your sides.

✦

No matter what
sort of difficulties,
how painful our
experience is, if
we lose our hope,
that's our real
disaster.

—LHAMO THONDUP
*Fourteenth Dalai Lama*

# Think Best-Case Scenario

Catastrophizing refers to a kind of thinking that fixates on the worst possible outcome, even when it's unlikely. It's a tendency that distorts any sense of possibility and hope. When you're stressed and anxious about the future or about how something will work out, try this.

1. Write down the absolute worst-case scenario. Don't just write down the first thought, keep asking yourself "And then what happens?" For example, you might worry about screwing up at work. And then getting written up. And then getting fired. And then being unable to pay rent. And then getting evicted. And then being made homeless. And then freezing to death on the streets. Find the absolute worst-case scenario when you hit rock bottom.

2. Next, write out the best-case scenario. Again ask yourself "And then what?" For example, you get noticed by management when your mistake exposes a bigger issue for the organization. You get a promotion. You celebrate by buying a lottery ticket. You win millions and travel the world. You meet the love of your life in Buenos Aires and live happily ever after.

3. Finally, write out the most likely scenario, again using the same process. Your boss understands your mistake and puts you on a development plan. You learn a lot and work hard to improve your performance.

4. Reflect on these scenarios. Notice if the train of catastrophizing is stopped by thinking about the other possibilities.

# Turn Despair Into Possibility

The opposite of hope is despair. It's giving up. It's feeling like you're powerless and helpless to change things. But just wishing and hoping won't be enough to counter despair. Hope isn't about throwing glitter on a pile of garbage. Work with despairing emotions by consciously developing what psychologists call "grounded hope." Rather than trying to will yourself to be more positive in the face of difficulties causing you to despair, grounded hope is about being realistic while building confidence in yourself to take action based on what is within your control and what's possible.

1. Think about the absolute worst-case scenario from the previous exercise.
2. Assign a probability to any part of your worst-case scenario out of ten. How likely is this to really happen? (One being most probable and ten being least probable.)
3. Create a plan. Think about what you would do if the probability is higher than you'd like and some of the worst comes to pass. How will you choose to react? Imagine the possibilities. What would you do after facing this challenge?
4. Notice if having a plan of action shifts how you feel about your future possibilities.

# Hope Backward

Hope is most often a future-facing endeavor. It's about wanting to move forward. But if you're always focusing on where you feel you've gone wrong in the past, this can be a barrier to how optimistic you feel about your future. Look back with this daily journaling exercise and take some time to see where you went right to renew your hope.

Every day, write down what has gone well and specifically what you are doing that is good. It doesn't have to be something large or grand, like a big success. It can be that you took care of the tasks you needed to. Made a meal that fed your family. Got to work on time. Planned your time well. Put the effort in. Where did you make a positive contribution? What are you doing well today? What's going right?

After doing this for a month, survey what you've identified and take stock of all the things that you're good at and where you make a difference. Reflect on these positives to cultivate a sense of control over your destiny and whatever is to come.

✦

# We must accept finite disappointment, but never lose infinite hope.

—DR. MARTIN LUTHER KING JR.
*American minister and activist*

# Embrace Some and Something

Things in life are rarely black and white. But with all-or-nothing thinking, it might feel like they are. This leaves no room for the spectrum of gray that makes up most of our actual reality: "I'm a *total* screw-up." "My friend *never* shows up for me." "I *always* have the worst luck." The extremes of thoughts that include words like *always* or *never* are often a distorted way of seeing things that clouds any possible sense of hope.

Relax your rigid thoughts. Hope is about being resourceful and creative. Write down or catch yourself whenever you find yourself expressing a thought with an all-or-nothing belief. Look at it critically. Try to come up with ten possible alternative beliefs for this thought. If you feel you always have bad luck, come up with ten times you had even the tiniest bit of good luck. When you hit four green lights in a row. When you found a dollar on the sidewalk. When you didn't need your umbrella. If coming up with ten is too difficult, push yourself and try fifteen! This is meant to be an exercise to flex your creative thinking and open up your sense of possibility.

# Forgive Yourself

Feelings of guilt or self-hatred will prevent you from seeing the hopeful side of how things could be different or better. Even as you choose to consciously develop a practice of hope, you will make mistakes. No one is perfect. Don't suffer twice. Don't let yourself feel both the pain of the difficulty as well as the pain of self-aversion. Write out what you hold against yourself so that you can see it clearly to let it go.

1. This can be a very difficult exercise, so find a place that you love, where you feel safe and at home.
2. Create two columns on a piece of paper.
3. In the left column, write out any judgment you have toward yourself—anything where you are against yourself or blame yourself.
4. Allow any emotions that might get stirred up in this exercise to arise.
5. Against every judgment, in the right-hand column, write: "I forgive myself."
6. Read out each statement to yourself, followed by saying out loud: "I forgive myself."
7. Notice how you feel when you forgive yourself rather than judge yourself.
8. You might end the exercise by tearing up or burning this paper, letting go of your judgments, ending any war you have with yourself, and being free.

# Anchor Yourself in the Present

When you feel something like anxiety or despair, you might be tempted to go to war with it. It's not a pleasant feeling, so you try to avoid it or "fix" it. You try to "just be positive!" But this can cause a struggle within you rather than lead to peace and hope. Try this meditation to start changing your relationship to the difficult feelings that arise and to work with the unpleasant thoughts, rather than trying to suppress them. As the saying goes, what we resist, persists. The mindful technique in Vipassana meditation might help you to work with whatever arises in the present moment.

1. Come into a comfortable meditation seat. Relax into your body as you close your eyes or rest your gaze softly in front of you to take your focus inward.
2. Notice what you can hear. Identify the farthest sound, perhaps outside of where you are sitting. Then, tune in to the closest sound around you.
3. Scan your body from your toes to your head, paying attention to any sensations you feel.
4. Take your attention to your breath. The subtle sound of it. The temperature. The feel of it and where it moves in your body on every inhale and exhale.
5. Take everything in that you experience in the present moment, not letting any one thing be bigger or more important than another. Anchor yourself here in your present experiences. Relax into what is.

✦

# Because you are alive, everything is possible.

—THICH NHAT HANH
*Buddhist monk and author*

# Spend Five Minutes in Complete Awe

If life is becoming dulled by routine and you are bored, you might lose sight of the magic all around you. Stir up a sense of hope by consciously choosing to stand in awe at nature.

Go outside, perhaps at dusk when the light is fading and casting colors on the grass, the leaves of the trees, the contours of the clouds that might be puffy in the sky full of pale blues, pinks, oranges, and mauves. Take in whatever is within your view with wonder. You might move from noticing the smallest things you can see, whether it be individual flowers, leaves, or buzzing insects, and move out toward the larger expanse, taking in full lampposts, houses, trees, fences, power lines, and fields. Take in your environment, and feel how wonderful it is that you are here, now, a part of it all.

# Imagine the Impossibilities

Few thoughts are as demotivating as wondering: What's the point? Life is full of so many possibilities, and at times it's important to remind yourself of all that this crazy life has to offer.

Create a bucket list of all the things you want to do before you die. Write down all the places you want to see. The things you want to create. Relationships you want to build. Ask yourself in particular what you've always wanted to do, but are scared to do. Maybe you have ambitions to write a book, start a video channel, go freelance, travel the world, or learn a language, but there are fears surrounding these dreams and you feel you can't have them. For this exercise, don't worry at all about the *how* of what you'll do. If it seems impossible for you, that's even more reason to add it to the list. Focus on the experiences you want to have more than the outcomes you want to see. This isn't about creating a plan to do these things. It's about realizing you have things you still want to experience. Notice how you feel while looking at your list. Come back to this list from time to time and see if there is anything you can cross off or add to it.

# Get Creative

Hope is, at its heart, a creative exercise. You need the imagination to want better or more or different. It's the art of the possible. Yet many people don't consider themselves creative at all. The truth is, everyone *is* creative. You merely might have lost the ability or forgotten it through regimented education and nine-to-five boundaries. Creativity is a skill rather than a born trait, which means you can learn and develop it! What's even better is that creativity is infinite. It really is. Start creating more than you consume. Get off the scroll of social media and make something.

Spend some time creating today. Find people doing creative work that you admire. You can even start by copying or emulating them. This can be part of relearning the creative process within you. Think of it like the difference between being a cook or being a chef. As a cook, you follow recipes. As a chef, you invent new flavors and tastes. There is nothing wrong with starting as a cook. That's how you learn! You'll master the skills and move on to tweaking a thing here and there as you like. Eventually, you could even create your own dishes. Give yourself permission to start and try to relax into your imagination.

✦

# Somewhere, something incredible is waiting to be known.

—CARL SAGAN
*American astronomer and author*

# Climb a Tree

When was the last time you climbed a tree? You might think this is kid's stuff. But there is a curiosity in children that sometimes gets lost with age. Returning to this sense of exploration can bring joy and hope with a new perspective.

Take a walk and find a tree. See if you can find one that's easily climbable. At the various heights you can reach, take in your surroundings and notice how your perspective changes. Can you see more of the horizon? More of the sky?

If you're not able to find a suitable tree or you're unable to do this one, simply sit under an inviting tree. Lean against the trunk for support and rest your head back on the texture of the bark. Look up, through the branches, to the sky and the clouds. Pause to notice every small change in the sway of the branches, the flight of the birds, the shift of the clouds. Slowing down is a beautiful way to shift your perspective toward hope.

# Give Yourself Permission

Do you feel that you don't deserve the things you want in life? Do you limit your hopes because you feel unworthy of them? Or does fear get in the way of letting yourself truly dream big? Perhaps you're not even aware of the ways you hedge against yourself. It might come easy to tell yourself "no" or "I can't" or "not right now."

What would you say to a child who told you about their hopes and dreams? Picture yourself as you were when you were a child. Imagine yourself somewhere that was special to you in childhood and where you felt safe. Ask your child-self what they want and what they hope for you in the future. Notice how you feel considering the hopes of this child-self compared to your adult-self. Acknowledge their wishes without limiting them. Take your child-like self in your arms and wrap these dreams in security.

# Put Down Your Devices

How many times do you pick up your phone or another electronic device in a day? There are statistics in your phone settings that will probably tell you, and it might surprise you just how tethered to your devices you are. It can become like an addiction. And, like any addiction, at best it doesn't add much good to your life and at worst it consumes all your attention so that none is left for better things.

Dedicate a day in your week to being device-free. You'll be forced to break the connection in your brain that wants to pick it up to see what you're missing. Fear of missing out gets in the way of hope because you're enslaved to things that are fear-based rather than what you truly want for yourself. Notice how you feel at the start of the day. It's natural to feel like something is missing or to feel anxious. Spend time throughout the day with your thoughts. Notice how you feel at the end of the day.

✦

# The garden of the world has no limits, except in your mind.

—RUMI

*Persian poet and Islamic scholar*

# Jump!

As you go through the motions of daily life and routine, you might not even see anymore what potentially unnecessary limits you have set yourself. Consider the metaphor of the jumping flea. For their size, fleas are some of the best jumpers out there. They can jump over 13 inches vertically in the air! But something happens if you put a flea in a jar with a lid on it. After the flea realizes it can only jump to the limit of the lid, it stops jumping altogether. It stops trying to escape its confines and forgets that jumping to great heights is an option.

Are you aware of the limits you're placing on your hopes and dreams? Ask yourself if there are ways you hold back in your desires. What do you really want but you say to yourself you can't have it? What do you hope for that fear stops, keeping your feet on the ground? How can you lift the lid and reach out for these yearnings?

# Cherish Your Gifts

It's hard to feel hopeful when you're hiding your light. Have you ever been told you're "too" something? Too sensitive. Too loud. Too passionate. Too much. And, in response, have you covered up these parts of yourself? Have you tried to be something you're not to please others? Have you dimmed your light to protect yourself from their judgment? When you're shot down for the things that inspire and touch you the most, it wounds a very core part of yourself. But it also points the way to identifying and understanding your greatest gifts. Resist the urge to abandon yourself. Uncover what you might have buried over the years in an effort to belong. Let down your defenses and embrace your authentic self by intentionally considering what shuts you down and what lights you up.

- Think of a time you suppressed your natural way of being because of someone else's judgment. How did this feel? Is there a way to consider this as a gift rather than a negative? For example, sensitivity can make you more attuned to the needs of others. Passion can give you energy to make an impact on a cause.
- Think of a time when you felt something deeply and your heart was filled. What was it about that experience that made you feel that way?
- Identify people in your life who support you and appreciate the gifts you bring. Ask them to tell you what they most respect and enjoy about you.

# Breathe In the Universe

Taking the burdens of life on by yourself is naturally going to be overwhelming. That's why a crucial ingredient for hope is connection. Try this breathing exercise as a reminder of how you are connected to everything. You are made of stardust, breathing in the exhales of the Earth and everyone who has ever lived.

Don't strain throughout this exercise. You don't need to suck in air to breathe. Breathing is a process having to do with the pressure within you and the pressure in the atmosphere outside your body. You make space and the universe fills it. You are connected to everything in it through this bridge in your breath.

1. Lie down somewhere comfortable on your back.
2. Take your hands to your belly. Breathe here, feeling the rise and fall of your stomach.
3. Take your hands to your chest. Notice here where the breath moves in you, expanding your ribs as your diaphragm moves.
4. Take your hands to your collarbone. Even here, where it might be more subtle, feel how your breath creates space, expands within you, and leaves you in a continual cycle.
5. Rest your hands and breathe making full use of your diaphragm, filling space in your collarbone, chest, and belly.

◆

Everything can be taken from a man but one thing: the last of the human freedoms— to choose one's attitude in any given set of circumstances, to choose one's own way.

—VIKTOR E. FRANKL
*Austrian psychiatrist and Holocaust survivor*

# Counter Resignation with Spontaneity

Resignation is a crisis of hope. It may lead to feelings of numbness that make you want to stay in bed all day. In some ways, it is the most difficult crisis of hope to deal with. When you feel despondent or hopeless, how do you even begin to develop a sense of possibility? Be kind to yourself when you're feeling this way. At the same time, see if you can jolt yourself into more action, even if it is tiny at first. If you're waiting to feel motivated, you'll be waiting an awfully long time. It's taking action that leads to feeling motivated, not the other way around. One way to tap into an antidote to resignation is to be spontaneous with these small tips.

- **Take a new route.** On your commute, a usual walk, or a drive somewhere you go often, take a new route to get there.
- **Break a routine.** Go out for breakfast on a weekday. Visit somewhere you've never been. Dance instead of watching TV. Ask a friend to come over. Say yes when you usually say no. Talk to a stranger.
- **Take a risk—do something that scares you.** Is there something you're avoiding doing out of fear? If you can identify a small feeling of fear, it's actually a good thing! It can mean not all hope is lost. You still care about something. Investigate what's holding you back and find the smallest next action you can take and do it now.

# Choose a Growth Mindset

There are often two mindsets one can use to look at life: a mindset of growth and opportunity, or a mindset that focuses on life's limitations. A limited mindset says things like: "I can't do this. I won't bother trying. It's not possible." A growth mindset says things like: "I might not know how to do this, but I can learn, ask for help, or find a way to make it possible in some way." A growth mindset is a hopeful mindset. The truth is that your potential and capabilities are unknown. They're not fixed and unmoving. You are capable of great change and growth, and it's your effort that determines this.

1. Write down something you want in your life, but that feels impossible for you.
2. Now write down all the excuses and reasons why you feel you can't have or do this thing.
3. Look at the reasons you've identified as holding you back or limiting you. See if you can flip any of these statements by writing them with a grain of possibility within them. Change "It'll never work" to "What if this works?" Change "I can't do it" to "I can learn." Or, add the word "yet" to the end of everything you've written down. "I don't have the resources—yet." "I can't figure out how to do this—yet."
4. Notice how your limitations look to you now. Is there space for the light of potential to enter?

# Ask a Guiding Question

If you feel conflicted or unsure about yourself, try this simple guiding question adapted from Kamal Ravikant. See if it resonates with what you're dealing with and provides any clarity or optimism about the way forward. This question is about being confident in yourself. It's about loving yourself and truly wanting the best for yourself. It takes this self-love as a starting point to make whatever you're dealing with more clear.

So here it is, say out loud to yourself: "If I truly believed in myself and that I deserve what I hope for, what would I do?"

Ask yourself if you truly loved yourself, would you let this happen? Would you allow yourself to be treated this way? Would you be okay with letting yourself experience this? Adapt the question based on whatever you're dealing with, but start from the assumption that you are worthy of everything good that you hope for yourself. Notice how this question makes you feel about what you're asking of it.

◆

# You are the sky. Everything else—it's just the weather.

—PEMA CHÖDRÖN
*American-Tibetan Buddhist nun*

# Enter a Haven of Hope

Hope can be like entering a kind of haven—a place where you feel truly safe and without anxiety about the future. This physical technique called "havening" is designed to facilitate this experience through touch rather than as a specific place or location, so that you can retreat from the chaos of life wherever you might be.

1. Sitting comfortably, first notice how you feel. Take your awareness to your breath.
2. Crossing your arms in front of you, take your hands to their opposite shoulder. Softly slide your palms down the outer edges of your arms, up and down. You might also say to yourself a mantra, such as "I am safe."
3. Next, take your hands in front of you, palm-to-palm. Slide your hands, taking your fingers down over your palm toward your wrist and up again. Repeat any mantra you are using.
4. Finally, take your fingers to your forehead and gently trace across your brow toward your temples. Say your mantra to yourself.
5. Rest your hands in your lap and notice how you feel. Repeat your mantra to yourself if you've used one.

# Sing a Song

There's a reason that some form of singing or chanting can be found in all major religions: Creating sound together attunes people to one another. As you mix your vocals with someone else's, you adjust slightly, almost like a radio dial finding a frequency. And when you find it, it creates a resonant sense of connection that can help you to transcend feelings of loneliness or despondency.

You don't have to be in a choir or have what you consider a good singing voice to benefit from this power. Simply pick a song that you love to sing, and sing it! Notice how you feel before you start singing and after. If you're on your own, you can still benefit from this in-the-moment release of breath and noise. You can also try playing a song on a device and sit facing it, singing toward it and harmonizing with the recording. Or, if you have a partner or friend to try this with, sing together and let your sound waves mingle and mix as you tune in to one other.

# Catch the Chatter

What were you just thinking about before you opened this book or read this sentence? Your mind is full of chatter. It runs along all day, and you don't always pay attention to each thought or the emotions that they bring, which can sometimes feel as though they come out of nowhere. To be more mindful of negativity and more aligned to the positive, try getting the thoughts out of your head and onto paper with a "morning pages" routine. Writing out your thoughts can help you let go of what's unhelpful and build greater awareness of the directions or loops your mind is running in.

1. Every morning, first thing, pull out some paper and a pen.
2. Write down whatever is in your head. Don't analyze it. Don't overthink it. Don't try to make it profound. If you're thinking about making coffee and that your nose itches a bit and that it's cold on your feet and where are your slippers, write those thoughts down. It's like you're transcribing your thoughts, rather than trying to direct them.
3. Continue to write for three full pages of whatever is coming to mind.
4. When you're done, put the pages away. Don't go back to them or reread them. Again, this isn't about creating something useful or interesting. It's simply to get the gunk out and let it go. Notice how you feel in doing so.

✦

# If we have our own "why" of life we shall get along with almost any "how."

—FRIEDRICH NIETZSCHE
*German philosopher*

# Fix Something

Most of us have them—a junk drawer, a back-of-the-closet, a basement box—a place where we store broken things that we think we'll one day fix. Because things are so cheap these days, there's a tendency to treat them cheaply—to throw away what breaks when it could easily be mended and saved from entering a landfill. Find something you stopped using because it's broken. It could be as simple as a sock or a sweater with a hole in it. Bust out the sewing kit and make it usable again! If you don't have anything that needs fixing, what can you upcycle? Make something old feel new again. This is a great exercise that is about working with what you have and making the best of things. Things don't always turn out as you'd hoped, but you can still make use of something rendered unusable or make something beautiful.

# Journal Your Joys

What made you happy today? When hope seems lost, it can seem like everything is gray. You might feel like there's no point to anything, while the world seems to be going on around you. Try this journaling exercise for one month as a way of orienting you to all the things, big and small, that bring you happiness in your life.

At the end of the day, write down everything that brought you joy that day. It could be something small; joy isn't always a sense of complete and utter awe or happiness. Look for moments where you felt content, at peace, and in flow.

At the end of the month, review what you've written. Are there any patterns? What kinds of things are making you happy? What can you do to bring more of these experiences into your life?

# Plant a Seed

Taking care of something or someone is a great source of resilience. It brings you outside of yourself as an individual and connects you to something bigger. This can be found in caring for others, volunteering, looking after a pet, or even something as simple as nurturing a seedling.

Plant an indoor window herb garden. Basil is an easy-to-grow herb that quickly becomes leafy. Not only can you watch it grow and thrive, but you can take satisfaction in producing something tasty that you can use in your own cooking sauces like pesto.

1. Soak the seeds in warm water overnight to help speed up their germination when you plant them.
2. Prepare a clean seedling tray. You can even recycle plastic yogurt containers for this—simply poke some holes in the bottom and place them on a plate.
3. Fill your container with soil or compost.
4. Make a small hole in the middle of your soil and drop a seed or two into each container, about ¼" deep. Gently cover them with soil.
5. Water the containers with a light sprinkle so that the seeds don't get displaced.
6. Keep the soil moist and watch for sprouts in five to ten days.
7. Plant the seedlings into larger pots when they're large enough to handle.

✦

However bad life may seem, there is always something you can do, and succeed at. While there's life, there's hope.

—STEPHEN HAWKING
*English theoretical physicist and author*

# Breathe Deep

Your breath is like a bridge between your mind and body. It's one of the few processes that is automatic but also under your direct control, like blinking. If you tend to hold a lot of tension in your body, taking some deeper breaths might help you to relax. Tension could be a sign you're on guard, watching out for whatever you fear is about to go wrong. Soften into hope with these diaphragmatic breathing tips.

1. Sit or lie down in a comfortable position.
2. Bring one hand to your belly and one hand to your chest, spreading the fingers of this hand so that they reach your collarbone.
3. Breathe naturally and notice where the breath moves in you. Is it more in your chest or belly? Can you feel even your collarbone moving?
4. Start to breathe more deeply. Concentrate on filling your belly, then your chest, then your collarbone area and then releasing on your exhale from your collarbone, to emptying your chest, to your belly.
5. Take ten breaths this way, filling and emptying. Release tension in your body with every exhale.

# Turn Around at Rock Bottom

Everyone has their own rock bottom. It's a relative concept, not an absolute one. This means that you very well might experience things in life that make you feel as though you can't sink any lower. You might feel you've failed or that you can't get back up and your hopes are dashed. It might not seem like a positive at first, but there is no such thing as security in life. Everything moves, everything is temporary, everything is subject to change. At any point, you are probably closer to rock bottom than you think.

But it's not all doom and gloom. There is hope, even at your lowest. There's a concept called post-traumatic growth, which means that, although it might not feel like it at the time, these challenges can expand you in ways you never even imagined. Much meaning in life is gained through how you struggle. It opens opportunity to determine what's important and what gives your life purpose.

How? Whatever you're going through, radically accept where you are. Don't fight against it. Then, take action, even if it's only one baby step. Finally, with each tiny move forward say to yourself the mantra: "I can become stronger through this."

# Find Good News

Certain things seem to loom larger than others, even when they're actually rare. For example, you might worry about plane crashes despite the fact that the data would show you're far more likely to face a car accident that never crosses your mind as you get behind the wheel every day. If the potential for world-rocking events is magnified in your mind, it can deplete your hope. But it's often only that these things *seem* more likely because they are unusual. The twenty-four-hour news cycle hypes this effect.

Notice how you feel when you consume the news sources you turn to in your life. Include your social media feed as an information source. Does it make you feel hopeful or worried?

You don't have to put your head in the sand, but you can choose what media you consume and proactively seek out good news. Unfollow or hide the sensationalized rare events and remind yourself of the positive. Silence or mute the conversations, debates, and channels that present only a bleak view of the world. Amplify the things that bring you joy. Notice how you feel when you suddenly have a newsfeed full of baking tips, yoga, inspirational writing, and creative content compared to speculative fear-based negativity.

✦

# Keep some room in your heart for the unimaginable.

—MARY OLIVER
*American poet*

# Write a Letter to Your Future Self

Hope isn't a vague, passive wish for things to work out or be better than they are right now. Hope is an active, positive outlook for your future self and who you are becoming.

Write a letter to yourself that you will open in exactly one year. You can use good old-fashioned pen and paper, tuck it in an envelope, and hide it somewhere you won't be likely to find it. Set yourself a reminder on a calendar to open it this time next year. Or, you can write it on your device of choice and use an online service like FutureMe, which will automatically email you the letter on your chosen date.

Consider what you hope for yourself one year from now. How do you hope you'll feel? What do you hope you'll have experienced this year?

Reflect, too, on where you are right now. What are you proud of from the last year? What will make you proud of yourself over the next year? What have you learned about yourself in the last year? What do you want to learn in the next year?

In a year, you can reflect on what you thought was important and what is important now. You might be surprised at how much you've changed, grown, and achieved for yourself when you take this time to listen to your past self.

# Deal with Disappointment

Hope is about wanting the best for yourself and aiming to be your best self. But there's a fine line between hope and expectation. Expectation can be based in entitlement. In a way, expectations are often inflexible. They lead to more fixed ideas of exactly how things should be. And this focus inevitably leads to disappointment because you have little actual control over the outcome of anything. Disappointment itself is a natural thing to feel. But when it strikes, it might help to look at what expectations lie underneath it.

Turn to face the disappointment you feel. Observe what you're feeling fully and then step back to see it with more objectivity. Where can you be proud of your effort? Where can you relax your expectations of how things should be and still have hope around the ultimate objective? Remember, this isn't the same as saying you shouldn't have high expectations for yourself or you need to see whatever has happened as a good thing. It's about letting go of rigid expectation and opening the door for your hopes to be fulfilled in ways you didn't even imagine.

# Become a God/dess

Your mental state impacts your body and you might not even be aware of it. This could show up as you hunch your shoulders, slouch your posture, and lower your head. It's difficult to feel powerful in your optimism when your body is signaling that it feels unsafe and unconfident. Try this yoga pose when you need to tap into a sense of your divine, to embody your inner god or goddess.

1. Standing, firmly plant your feet wider than your hips, with your toes facing outward at about a 45 degree angle.
2. Extend your arms straight out beside you. Your feet might be under your wrists in this position. Make any adjustments you need to for this wide stance.
3. Bending at your knees to about 90 degrees, sink down so that your thighs become parallel to the ground. Keep your thighs pressing outward and your spine tall rather than leaning forward. At the same time, bend at your elbows so that your upper arms remain parallel to the ground, but your forearms and hands are perpendicular as your fingertips reach up toward the ceiling.
4. Hold this shape for five rounds of breath.
5. Press up strong through your heels and thighs to come back up to standing and release your arms.
6. Notice how you feel and see if you can take strength with you into the rest of your day.

✦

You have not grown old, and it is not too late

To dive into your increasing depths

Where life calmly gives out its own secret.

—RAINER MARIA RILKE
*Austrian poet and novelist*

# Change Your Mind

Are you a pessimist or an optimist by nature? Do you believe you can become more optimistic? You are a combination of your genes and your environment, and these two factors shape you through your life experiences. But you're not an unchanging, fixed personality. Your brain is "plastic," which means it has the capability of creating and forging new connections. Even the simple act of reading a book will change you forever, though it might be in very small ways! More of your thoughts than you'd initially suspect are habitual and repeated; the brain is a pattern-making machine, which gives you shortcuts to work in day-to-day living. You can forge new patterns. It takes effort. This is not a simple process. But it is perhaps the most hopeful one there is—the way you view the world is your reality, but you have the power to change it, like switching a lens on a camera. Mindful meditation helps to build on this ability and there are specific therapies that use the power of neuroplasticity to create change. Try these tips to increase your mind power more generally.

- Travel or visit somewhere you've never been where all the sights and sounds around you are new and you need to pay attention.
- Spend some time every day with a memory game or mind puzzle.
- Learn a new language or how to play a musical instrument.
- Make sure you are getting enough quality sleep.

# Learn Something New

Feeling hopeless can make you wonder what the point is in anything. A potent antidote to this can be found in learning something new. Learning is a process of growth and self-expansion. It's growing hope in action. And yet many people fall out of love with learning after experiencing rigid and boring education systems. There's a difference between education and learning. Education is often a formal system with a syllabus and an evaluation. Someone else dictates what you need to learn and tests you on it. Learning, on the other hand, can be purely self-directed. It can have a more direct use in helping you solve a problem or make something you care about.

Take some time to learn something new that lights you up. There are many open online courses you can now take offered by different universities or from people sharing their skills. Find something you want to know more about. Find something that doesn't feel like "work" or old-school education. When you lose track of time, you know you're on to something that speaks to you that you can spend time with. Let learning expand you and you'll never be the same.

# Get Your Heart Beating

When you need some energy, get your heart working. High-intensity interval training, also known as HIIT, sounds like an intense workout, and it can be. But it's also something you can do at home, even if all you have is a few minutes. Try it to feel your heart beating in your chest. It's a reminder that you are alive, now, and life is full of possibilities.

Set a timer that you can see. Do each exercise for twenty seconds and give yourself a ten-second pause between each one. Or, start with a lower ratio, such as exercising for fifteen seconds and taking a sixty-second break. Work where your body is comfortable and you'll build endurance over time.

- Jumping jacks. Jump your feet out wide while raising your arms out to the side and up overhead.
- Squat. Bending at your knees, sink your bum down toward the ground, using the strong power of your legs to push yourself back to standing.
- Run on the spot.
- Lunge. Take one foot forward and lower down until both knees are bent about 90 degrees before you press back up and alternate with the other side.
- Hop. Hop with both feet forward and backward, increasing the distance you jump as you go.
- Push-ups. From a plank position, with knees lowered if you'd like, lower yourself down, bending at your elbows, and push yourself back up to your starting position.
- Run on the spot with high knees, taking your knees up to about hip level.

✦

And the day came
when the risk to
remain tight in
a bud was more
painful than the risk
it took to blossom.

—ANAÏS NIN
*French-Cuban writer*

# Take a Self-Portrait

Selfies are a modern-day obsession, but with filters and unrealistic beauty standards they can make you feel as though you don't measure up. However, choosing how you want to present your face to the world can also be empowering if you own what you want to convey in the photo. Think less about impressing others and meeting their standards, and more about what you love about yourself that you want to share.

Go beyond the standard selfie and take a self-portrait. Use the self-timer function or get a friend to help you. Create this portrait in a place that you love. Perhaps it's at home, in your favorite cafe, or in nature. Wear your favorite outfit that makes you feel confident. Think about what else you want in the shot and surround yourself with some of your favorite things and things that tell a story about you and what you care about. Think about what kind of mood you want to imbue with self-confidence. You don't even have to share this photo. Make it about expressing something, which could be just for you, to remember this time in your life and what you love about you.

# Shift Helpless to Hopeful

Did you know you can learn to be helpless? Learned helplessness is a kind of unconscious process. It's like a dog that has been conditioned to not go near an electrified fence. The dog knows it will shock her, so she stops going near it, even after she's able to leave without a shock. You learn certain behaviors and ways of responding in your life that are adaptive to the situation you're in. Curling up in a ball might have helped you to de-escalate abuse or confrontations. The problem is that you might continue to use these learned behaviors even when they no longer serve you. It's a very damaging result because an ability to feel in control of your own life is key to resilience. But there's hope. You can unlearn behaviors when you're aware of what they are. When you face a difficult situation, try this ABC reframing technique developed by Dr. Albert Ellis and Dr. Martin Seligman.

- **Adversity.** Describe the situation you faced.
- **Belief.** What kind of story are you telling yourself about this situation? How did you interpret things?
- **Consequences.** How did you handle the situation? What do you normally do in these situations?
- **Disputation.** Is your first instinct and reaction useful in dealing with the situation? What are the possible results of following through as usual?
- **Energization.** Refocus on responding to this situation in a way that serves you. Notice how it feels to interrupt your usual patterns and be in control of how you respond.

◆

When you change
the way you look at
things, the things
you look at change.

—DR. WAYNE DYER
*American author and speaker*

# Flip Your Switch

Two people experience the same event but can respond very differently. One person sees a lost job or relationship as a devastating ending, whereas another sees it as an opportunity to pursue something new that they've been putting off. One person succumbs to self-pity and defeat, and another uses it as fuel to be resilient and grow stronger. You can choose which perspective you adopt. It might not feel like it, but the only difference between these two experiences is in how each person decides to see it.

When you face difficulty in your life, even in the small ups and downs of a day, ask yourself which perspective you're adopting: defeat or development. Whenever you notice you are trending toward defeat, social worker and author Christian Moore suggests you ask yourself how you can flip the switch on your perspective. Flip from pessimistic to optimistic. Flip from limitation to growth. Flip from failure to potential. Notice how you feel when you do. Remember, you're not denying bad or sad feelings if that's what you are experiencing. But you're looking at the meaning and story you construct around the difficulty and ensuring it doesn't limit you unnecessarily, but expands you.

# Be Hopeless

In a book about hope, why would it make sense to think about embracing hopelessness? According to Buddhist nun and author Pema Chödrön, true freedom lies in being hope*less*. What does this mean? Because hope is about what you want in the future, it could be used as an escape from the present moment and any pain and suffering you are facing. But in Buddhist teachings, suffering is part of life. You can't escape this fact, but you can learn to work with it. If your impulse is to solve and fix things, hope can be a kind of never-ending disappointment as you grasp at these projects. Try these meditation instructions to relax into what is, exactly as it is.

Sit comfortably, close your eyes or rest your gaze, and take your awareness to your breath, breathing in and out through your nose. Keep your focus on your breath throughout your meditation.

Whatever arises in your thoughts and feelings, see if you can let them be. If difficult emotions and thoughts come, give yourself permission to feel them. Know that you're safe where you sit in meditation and you can tolerate these fluctuations. Know that you can't eliminate pain and adversity from your life. Release the need to ruminate on where you went "wrong" in the belief that you could avoid making any mistakes or being hurt again. Love whatever arises as part of your human experience. Know it will ebb and flow—nothing is permanent. It's not about finding negative feelings and replacing them with positive ones. This practice is about letting everything that is part of your experience be with you, as it is.

✦

# Hope is a
# waking dream.

—ARISTOTLE

*Greek philosopher*

# Sleep On a Problem

If something is bothering you and preventing you from seeing the sunny side of things, try this journaling exercise.

1. Before you go to sleep, write down what you're struggling with. Get everything you can onto the page about this problem or situation that is tripping you up and how you feel about it.
2. Go to sleep, knowing that you've released the problem onto the page and you are now going to rest free of this issue. You don't need to worry about it because you've spent the time getting it out of your head.
3. When you wake up the next morning, jot down ideas about how you could approach this issue. What can you change or what actions can you take? Could you change how you see this problem? What other perspective could you take that would change how you feel about it? Notice if a fresh pair of rested eyes helps you to see this in new ways.

# Chant with the Universe

When you're struggling to find your place in the world, give this exercise a try that is all about connecting from the inside out. Chanting provides a deep vibration that connects your body to the world around you via the sound waves you create. One such chant, "Om," is said to be the sound of the universe—the sound when it all began. Use this chant of hope to see that there is a plan for you and where you fit in the universe.

1. Breathe in and out from your nose slowly. Listen to the subtle sound of the breath as it enters your nostrils and as it leaves you.
2. Take a deep breath in through your nose.
3. On the exhale, open your mouth slightly and breathe out while creating a sound deep in your throat for "Om." You can simply say *Ooommmm*, or you can transition in different parts of the sound. Om is often made up of four sounds. Start with an *aaaah*, move to an *ooooh*, and end by closing your lips and saying *mmmm*. The fourth sound is actually the brief silence at the end of the chant.
4. Repeat this inhale, exhaling "Om" for several rounds. Feel the vibration within you, in your throat, between your lips.
5. Notice how you feel. Try this exercise sitting across from someone else or in a group sitting close together in a circle, feeling the sound waves mingling, washing over you and connecting you.

# Let the Light In

When you feel crushed by the weight of despair, you need to consciously open up to the light—to choose hope. A visualization can help you do this in the abstract, which might also bring light to your mindset and whatever it is you face.

1. Lie down comfortably and close your eyes.
2. Count backward from three: "three, two, one."
3. Imagine you are in a dark room. You can barely see your hand in front of your face. But you can see a tiny crack of light in a window in one of the walls.
4. Walk toward the window. On the windowsill, you barely make out the contours of a clean rag.
5. See yourself pick up the rag and clean the window, brushing off the dust and dirt. Light begins to naturally pour into the room until you can see everything around you. You can even look out the window now, to a beautiful landscape.
6. Count up to three: "one, two, three."
7. Pay attention to how you feel now.

✦

Only when we
are brave enough
to explore the
darkness will we
discover the infinite
power of our light.

—BRENÉ BROWN
*American professor and author*

# Create a Compliment List

Dashed hopes, anguish, and desperation can be enough to deal with on their own. But these are made even worse if you turn against yourself. You know it's not true, but you can suddenly feel worthless and hopeless. It's as if nothing you've ever done is worth anything and you're the worst person to have ever lived. Rationally, you know this isn't true, but it can be difficult to see it or convince yourself of it when you're in negative rumination.

Start keeping track of compliments you receive from people when you receive them. Create a document in your computer or in a paper notebook where you can jot down what people say about you. Start to notice when people thank you for something or when they tell you you're good at something. You could even get it started by asking a few close people in your life what they like about you. Return to this list when you're feeling low as a reminder of all that you bring into the world. Pick out one or two things and remember them like a mantra you can say to yourself when you need to draw on a little extra positivity toward yourself and your efforts.

# Free Your Emotions

When strong emotions get the better of you, it can be tough to maintain hope. The technique in this practice, called emotional freedom, is a form of therapy that can help you diffuse big feelings when they arise, catch anxiety in the moment, and interrupt this response in your mind and body to return you to a state of calm. Here's how it works.

1. Notice how you're feeling in the moment. Investigate in your body where this feeling is showing up. It could be tightness in your chest or between your eyes, a clenched jaw, or pain or tension somewhere else in your body.
2. Take your attention to the feeling in your body. Notice its edges. Is it constant or does it fade or change as you focus on it?
3. With your fingers, lightly tap on the area of your body where you feel any sensations related to the feeling. Notice if this action changes the sensation and what you can tolerate.

# Relax with Restorative Yoga

Take some time to relax and restore. You might only be familiar with the higher intensity forms of yoga and envision people in handstands on the beach when you think of the practice. But yoga is really about a mind-body connection. It's a meditative practice. It doesn't have to be an exercise that works your muscles at all! Often called restorative yoga, these poses are about relaxing into your body and mind. With a relaxed body, you might be better able to cope with any challenges you face. Try these before bed and they might help you ease into sleep too.

In each of these shapes, sink into the support of the pillows or ground. Let every part of your body relax, releasing any tension in your jaw or forehead. Stay in each shape for at least five minutes.

1. **Fold forward.** Kneeling on the floor with your knees wide and big toes touching, pile a few long pillows up in front of you, between your knees. Fold your belly forward to rest on the pillows. Turn your head to one side, but make sure you switch sides halfway through.
2. **Elevate.** Find a chair, couch, bed, or stack of pillows that comes up to about knee-height for you. Lie down on your back and place your ankles and shins onto this support. Your legs will be bent around 90 degrees. This is a supported inversion.
3. **Open.** Lying on your back, stretch out long and place a pillow under your knees. This can help alleviate pressure in your lower back and allow you to relax.

✦

The appearance
of things changes
according to the
emotions; and thus
we see magic and
beauty in them,
while the magic and
beauty are really in
ourselves.

—KAHLIL GIBRAN
*Lebanese-American writer, poet, and artist*

# Manage Uncertainty

Anxiety about the future is the exact opposite of hope for the future. Anxiety is often about "what if." What if something bad happens. What if this doesn't turn out the way I want. What if I can't handle it. What if I screw it up. Uncertainty is really uncomfortable. Your brain might try to deal with it by envisioning every possible outcome. Hope, on the other hand, is without worry. It relies on trust. It's about what *is*. It's creative and innovative rather than fearful and anxious. It knows that whatever happens, you will adapt and be okay.

Catch yourself when you find a "what if" thought coming up. When you are "what if-ing" into unhelpful territory, come back to what is. Recognize it for the attempt at controlling uncertainty that it is. The thing is, this attempt to control also takes out key facets of hope, like surprise, delight, and curiosity. Find freedom in uncertainty. Let go of what if and ground yourself in what is.

# Know When to Fold 'Em

Hope is a neutral phenomenon. That is, you can hope for positive things that are good for you, but you can also hope for negative things that aren't necessarily helpful for you. How can this be?

There's a concept called "intermittent rewards" in psychology. When you get something you want, but it's randomly given, you are primed to keep trying to get it. Gambling is a great example. A person sitting at a slot machine keeps pulling the handle in the hope they'll win big. They win a little bit on one round and it keeps them going, even though on balance they're losing. Being in a push-pull relationship, where affection is given in one moment and taken away in another, is another devastating example. You stick around hoping for the times where love is given and are willing to suffer through the times where it's not while you wait for that reward. The very inconsistency of the affection keeps you glued to working for it. Your hope is used against you through manipulation and abuse.

Break the cycle of hoping for something that will never fully come to you. Track the patterns. Don't let the sporadic reward lead to ignoring all the times your needs aren't being met. Notice where you're accepting something in the hope that it will get better. Make a plan of action to go after what you need.

◆

# The boundary to what we can accept is the boundary to our freedom.

—TARA BRACH
*American psychologist and author*

# Dance Like There's No Limit

Ecstatic dance is a practice of letting your body move exactly as it feels like doing. Many forms of movement are about following regimented steps. But freedom can be found in letting loose. It's a moving meditation that brings hope with joy.

Put on some of your favorite music in a place where you can be alone. No one is watching you. It doesn't matter what you look like, so you can really go inward and focus on how you feel. You can surrender to whatever movement your body wants to make, regardless of how it looks. If you're struggling to get started, consider trying the five rhythms approach listed here.

1. Flow. Move continuously, flowing your arms, your spine, your head, your legs.
2. Take control. Make staccato, jerky movements, from your elbows, your wrists, your knees. Stop and start, with sharp moves.
3. Allow for chaos. Be wild, playful, move wherever the rhythm takes you. Release energy out your fingertips.
4. Slow down. Take your time, move slowly and softly.
5. Enter stillness. Notice how your body feels now.

# Visualize Your Dream Future

Visualizing what you want for your life is a powerful exercise of hope for your future. To picture what you want means you need to be clear on what that is. And, when you're clear, you'll be more likely to take action to realize your dream and to see opportunities that take you toward it. Commit to this exercise for seven days and notice how the picture develops and how you feel imagining this future for yourself.

1. In a quiet place, close your eyes and count out loud to yourself backward from three: "three, two, one."
2. Imagine yourself sitting in a theater watching a screen. On the screen you see your ideal future play out like a scene in a movie. Watch it play with as much detail as you can. Where are you? Who are you with? How do you feel? What are you doing?
3. When you feel like the scene has come to an end and you're ready to return, count out loud to yourself up to three: "one, two, three." Blink your eyes open.

# Go with the Flow

Hope is a fickle force. You need to draw on hope when you're low or you'll slip into despair. But at the same time, if you cling too desperately to the way you think things should go, you create rigid expectations and set yourself up for more disheartening disappointment. Find balance in going with the flow of hope with this visual meditation.

1. Imagine you've fallen into a fast-flowing river. You have two options.
2. Envision option one. Imagine you try to hold on to the shore. You grab a branch from an overhanging tree, but it slips from your fingers, cutting up your hands. You try to swim to get closer to the sides, but you hit boulders and rocks and bump and bruise your body in the shallows. You grasp at the ground of the riverbank, but your hands slip as the mud gives way.
3. Now picture option two. Imagine yourself pushing off to the middle of the river. Notice that the water here is clear and deep. You aren't hitting yourself on anything. You can swim here, keeping your head high and seeing what is ahead. You let the current carry you without resisting it.
4. Notice how each scenario feels to you. Place your hope in the flow of the middle of the river. Trust it will carry you to where you need to go, without you grasping and trying to direct its course.

✦

# Nothing should be out of the reach of hope. Life is a hope.

—OSCAR WILDE
*Irish writer*

# Turn Self-Doubt Into Self-Honor

Have you ever felt you should feel a certain way or be something other than who you are? Or that you shouldn't feel something you feel or be as you are? Self-doubt is rooted in a lack of trust in your authentic self. It comes from focusing more on the judgments of others than your own internal wisdom. It asks: "What's wrong with me?" You have no firm ground to place your hopes when you doubt yourself. Shift self-doubt to self-honor with the A-HA method.

1. **(Be) Authentic.** Recognize and name what you feel. Don't judge it or tell yourself you shouldn't feel it or you should feel something else. Simply be honest with what you are feeling.
2. **Honor what you really feel.** Ask yourself where this feeling has come from. In what ways does it make sense you'd feel this way? Dig deep. Keep in mind it might not be about the situation at hand, but a trigger from something else you are being reminded of now.
3. **(Take) Action.** What is this feeling asking of you? What do you want to do about it? Allow yourself to take care of your deeply felt vulnerabilities.

# Believe All Is Coming

You might know deep down exactly what you hope for, but you might not have the belief that it will come to pass. Dr. Wayne Dyer spoke about the need to be careful with your thoughts because what you think is what you are. If you constantly focus on what's missing in your life, you'll only continue to see what's missing. However, if you consciously think about what you want to attract, you will start to see the opportunities and possibilities that move you toward these desires.

Dyer proposed a perfect mantra to remember when you find yourself in a craving state that will bring you into a hopeful one instead: "It's on its way." With this mantra, you relax your doubts, you let go of thinking of it as a lack or something missing from your current life, and you develop a belief that it's simply not here yet, but it will come.

# Howl at the Moon

Okay, this isn't literally about howling at the moon. Unless of course you really need a release, then go for it! This is more of a symbolic howl at the moon. It builds on the idea that, although you don't have exactly what you hope for now, it's on its way. Perhaps it's a relationship or deep friendship that's missing. Perhaps you're searching for meaning and purpose. Perhaps you dream of getting to a new place or of having new means at your disposal.

Go outside at night when the moon is full and visible. The beautiful moon at its fullest is a perfect anchor in the sky to release all of your thoughts of what's missing. Imagine that someone else is also looking up at this moon tonight—they're just not here beside you yet. Somewhere, this moon is shining in a place you want to go to that you simply haven't arrived at yet. Someday, this moon will renew itself as your situation also renews itself. Let this light shine on your face and brighten you with the belief that it will come.

✦

I urge you to please
notice when you are
happy, and exclaim
or murmur or think
at some point, "If
this isn't nice, I
don't know what is."

—KURT VONNEGUT
*American writer*

# Be Grateful

Gratitude is a potent antidote to gloom. Take some time to meditate with an attitude of gratitude to unlock a more positive state of being in the moment.

1. Come to sit comfortably for meditation in a quiet place where you won't be interrupted.
2. Close your eyes and take your focus to the sound of your breath.
3. Check in with how you feel in your body and notice any places where you're holding tightness or tension.
4. Take for your focal point, the mantra: "I am grateful." You can make it more specific if you want, perhaps in gratitude for the relationships you have in your life, the challenges that have made you who you are today, the present moment and all that you can experience.
5. Anytime your mind wanders, come back to this mantra of gratitude and relax in your body.
6. Notice how you feel as you blink your eyes open at the end of your meditation. Resolve to greet the positive and the negative with gratitude for all both experiences offer in guiding and shaping you.

# Be Mindful in the Everyday

Meditation is about more than the time you spend sitting with your eyes closed watching your thoughts or bringing your attention to your focal point. It's actually about how the skills you build in this practice translate outside of the meditation itself into greater mindfulness during your daily life. Mindfulness helps you to respond rather than react. It helps you to be in control of where you put your attention. It gives you more distance and objectivity to the swirling thoughts and emotions that might otherwise carry you away. And all of these skills can help you to be more present and have a more positive outlook. Find moments throughout your day that you can use to serve as a reminder to yourself to take time for a mindful moment, such as through these examples:

- Brushing your teeth
- Waiting in line
- Eating a meal
- Drinking a cup of coffee
- Savoring a piece of chocolate
- Driving to work

# Write a Thank-You Letter

Spreading joy and hope to someone else in your life is likely to also increase the joy and hope that you feel. Take the time to send someone you appreciate a thank-you letter. These days the norm is quick correspondence by electronic means, such as email and texts. A paper letter is a great way to show someone they're special and have had an impact on you.

Think of someone who has helped you recently or been a positive influence in your life. What is it about them that you appreciate? What is it that they've done for you? It can be specific, like supporting your career with a reference or having you over for dinner last week. Or, it can be something more long term, like being there for you as a friend over the years. Take the time to tell them what you love about them and the impact they have had on your life. Notice how you feel as you pop the letter into the mail.

✦

Disasters shake things loose. And the things that we regarded as fixed and unchangeable can suddenly be changed.

—REBECCA SOLNIT
*American writer*

# Get Into Balance

Cultivating a hopeful outlook won't mean that every day is full of optimism. Each day is different and each day you should ask what hope needs of you now. Remind yourself to check in by trying a balancing yoga pose. Balancing poses are a challenge. You might feel in control and powerful and perfectly balanced one day and be wobbling all over the next. Finding balance has its own ebbs and flows because nothing truly stands still. Try the variations of this tree shape as you reflect on how you feel today. You might want to start next to a wall so that you can use your hand against it for extra support.

1. Standing with your feet hip-distance apart, slowly shift your weight to your left foot and peel your right foot off the ground, first lifting your heel and then picking up your toes.
2. Turning your right knee out to the side, place the sole of your right foot against your left ankle. Your toes can touch the ground here as you find balance.
3. Take your palms together in front of your chest or raise your arms up overhead while keeping your shoulders drawing down away from your ears.
4. To increase your balancing challenge, try placing your right foot against your left calf or inner thigh. Press your leg and foot into each other to create stability.
5. Repeat on the other side, standing on your right foot and taking your left foot up.
6. Be present with every wiggle. Work at whichever point you can to create stability, smooth out the wobbles, and find balance.

# Do Something for Your Cause

Don't let your hope be the waiting kind. You could hope that technology will swoop in to save the day or that someone else will fix what's wrong in the world. *You* are someone else. No one is coming—it's up to you. You can't tackle a big problem yourself. But you can join with others. You can take the smallest action toward a cause you care about and it will move the needle. Be the change you want to see. Here are some ideas how.

- Join a litter-picking group in your local park to prevent trash from clogging up waterways and damaging wildlife.
- Clean a section of beach to remove plastic that washes up. Take the plastic out of circulation in lakes, rivers, and the ocean where it harms fish and plants.
- Make a change in your life to something that is more sustainable and generates less waste. Cycle rather than drive. Take your canvas bags to the grocery store. Consume less and repair more.
- Plant a tree or garden in your community.
- Join a protest or speak out about something important to you.
- Stand up for someone else who is being bullied.
- Donate to a cause you believe in.
- Learn something new and educate yourself on an important topic so you can be an example to others and help to inform them as well.

# Trust You Are Provided For

Uncertainty can lead to intense experiences of fear and anxiety. And when you live in fear, there isn't much room for the light to get in. Uncertain times don't mean that the worst will happen—they could just as easily mean the best is yet to come. When you're worried and wondering what's coming, have faith. Trust that whatever happens, there is a place for you. That there will always be a way forward. That you will be taken care of, one way or another.

In meditation, or wherever you sit as you read this, inhale and gather in with your breath any doubts and uncertainties and fears. Exhale slowly, saying to yourself, "I am provided for." Relax and soften into the mantra as you do so, releasing your fears about what's uncertain. Imagine you are forging a diamond within you in this process, taking in everything negative, tumbling it within your body as the breath moves in you, smoothing the rough edges and revealing something strong and light and beautiful.

✦

# And I say to myself: a moon will rise from my darkness.

—MAHMOUD DARWISH
*Palestinian poet and author*

# Breathe for Calm under Stress

It's difficult to maintain a grounded sense of optimism when you're under pressure. The weight of stress can take over and leave you feeling crushed. When it all seems a bit much, try this breathing technique, popularized in the military, which can help to reduce your stress response and bring you back into a relaxed focus on what matters.

1. Rest your body in a way that you can feel comfortable, either sitting or lying down.
2. Notice how you are breathing now. Is it shallow or deep? Is it in your chest or is your whole diaphragm engaged? Is it fast? Or slow and measured?
3. Start slowing down the four parts of your breath. Notice your inhale, the slight pause you need to take at the top of it before you turn to exhale, your exhale, and the slight pause at the bottom as you turn to inhale once again.
4. Inhale to a count of four.
5. Pause for a count of four, holding your breath.
6. Exhale to a count of four.
7. Pause with the breath emptied from your lungs for a count of four.
8. Complete at least five rounds of this four-part box breath.
9. Let your breath return to a natural rhythm and notice how it feels compared to when you began.

# Forget Regret

Regret can help you to focus on things you want to do differently or areas of your life you want to change. But living in regret is like walking into a dark cave with the light source behind you getting fainter and fainter the deeper you go. Regret overshadows hope. It keeps you looking backward to the past at the expense of both your present and future. You feel things should have been different in some way and so it's impossible to enjoy where you are now. And you fixate on what might have been rather than on what could still be. Hope is forward-looking. Learn what you can from your inevitable mistakes, disappointments, and heartaches.

If you're kicking yourself for things you did or didn't do in the past, try asking yourself these questions to gain some perspective.

- What did you learn?
- What will you do differently now?
- How has this experience changed you?
- What did you learn about yourself?

# Focus On What You Can Control

Sometimes it can seem as if the world is getting darker and darker. Empathy is a beautiful gift, but when you take on the pain of the world it can feel like too much for one person to handle. And that's because, well, it is. You might not be able to put the world to rights overnight on your own. But you can make a difference. Peace and hope start from within and shine outward, lighting whatever they touch.

Consider this story of a yogi who was frustrated at having found tools that could heal, and yet still finding the world full of wars and poverty and conflict. At hearing his complaints, his guru tells him that he's been given a broom to clean his closet and yet is seeking to clean the entire world. He is instructed to clean his closet first and then go from there.

The thing is, you can't control everyone else. You can't control what your neighbor does, or your boss, or your spouse, or your president. It will cause you greater pain to try. What you *can* do is be an example. Live from your own truth. Focus on what is in your control. In psychology it's called an "internal locus of control." It means knowing what is in your influence and focusing there, releasing what is out of your hands while also not losing faith in your ability to have an impact. When things seem too big, identify what's in your control and take action there.

✦

When you arise in the morning think of what a precious privilege it is to be alive—to think, to enjoy, to love.

—MARCUS AURELIUS
*Roman emperor and philosopher*

# Create a Dream Collage

A good old-fashioned mood board can serve you with a daily visual reminder of what it's all for. Source some old magazines that you can cut up. Leaf through these and cut out any images that speak to you, move you, or make you happy. Include things that remind you of what you love from your past or things that are great about your present. And keep adding to it with things that you find that represent what you hope for in your future. On a large poster-sized board, start pinning or gluing these images that mean something to you. Place your board somewhere prominent where you'll see it every day. When you pass by it, make sure you pause at some point regularly. Take in how you feel looking at these things that have made your life great so far and all the things you are working toward.

# Act Like an Optimist

Is your M.O. to avoid? When things hit the fan, do you drop and run? It might seem counterintuitive, but optimists are good at facing problems rather than avoiding them. It's not that they tackle the difficulty with the magic of positive thoughts alone. It's that they don't bury their head in the sand and instead identify things for what they are so that they can take action to address the issue. Optimists are more likely than pessimists to see the situation as a challenge rather than a threat. And a challenge can be overcome. You need to seek information and walk toward the problem rather than away from it. So consider positive thinking as less about redressing the very real problem before you in positive terms, and more about positively thinking through what you want to do about it. Act like an optimist—face the problem head-on and take action.

# Tell a Story of Self-Compassion

When you face something difficult in your life it can be hard enough to deal with the situation at hand. But often there is a second wound that accompanies difficulty, where you blame yourself for what has happened. Blame can shut you down rather than open you up to the way forward in hope. Instead, practice compassion for yourself. Think of it like the Buddhist metaphor of the two arrows. If you've been struck by an arrow, this is a physical injury. But the second arrow is the mental injury you add to the first with the story that you tell. That it wasn't fair. That you deserved it. That it was just your luck. Don't suffer twice with a problem or difficulty you face. Allow yourself to make mistakes and still hold yourself in love. Wrap your arms around yourself in a hug as you breathe deeply and say out loud to yourself, "I am worthy."

✦

# It's not about what it is, it's about what it can become.

—THEODOR GEISEL (DR. SEUSS)
*American children's writer and illustrator*

# Visit a Sacred Place

When you're down, it might help you to create hope by changing your environment. The awe and wonder that a sacred place instills could be the inspiration you're looking for. This might be a spiritual or religious building such as a temple, church, mosque, or synagogue. It could be a community center or a yoga class. It might be an art gallery full of expression and creation, or a museum full of history and natural beauties. Try standing in the blue light of an aquarium watching jellyfish drifting or go to the top of a mountain with limitless views in all directions. Is there a spot that fills you with a feeling of awe and of being connected to others who feel the same in that place? Stand in this place and let these shared experiences of humanity fill you and give you the energy you need to keep going.

# Open a Box of Hope

The myth of Pandora is a story about how necessary hope is to conquer the difficulties of life. Pandora was given a box with a warning not to open it. Of course, naturally her curiosity got the better of her and she opened it, only to find that in doing so, she released the evils of the world including things like sickness and death. She quickly tried to close the box. Remaining inside was one last thing—hope. There are mixed interpretations of the tale as to whether hope remained as a necessary thing to keep in your heart to combat the evil that is in the world, or whether, more pessimistically, it too is a double-edged sword—an expectation that is a curse rather than a blessing. Let this story be a basis to reflect on where you place your hopes. Are they tied to rigid or shallow expectations? Or is it a well of belief in yourself that you can draw on to tackle the adversity you face?

# Paint the Color of Your Hope

If life seems dark, splash some color on it—literally. You'll need some paint and paintbrushes and something to paint on, whether it's a canvas, paper, or even some strong cardboard. Spend an hour moving paint onto the canvas. Bring something into being that expresses how you feel. You don't need to feel you have any creative skills for this. (Although, you *do* have creative skills even if you don't feel you do!) This is about expression. What colors best represent how you feel right now? What colors feel like they represent your hope? Use the brush as an extension of your arm and an extension of your feeling. If your feeling dictates long sweeping strokes, do that. If it requires more dabs or building up in splotches, listen to these impulses. You might splatter or swirl. See what it feels like to let go, to experience the color. Notice how you feel looking at what you've created.

✦

People grow through experience if they meet life honestly and courageously. This is how character is built.

—ELEANOR ROOSEVELT
*American diplomat and first lady of the United States*

# Build Post-Traumatic Growth

Hope doesn't mean that life will be smooth sailing if only you cling to it. Rather, hope requires you to keep sailing through the storm because you know that if you make it, you will appreciate the blue skies all the more. Light needs darkness. Meaning requires difficulty. It's within this meaning that hope thrives. People who have known great sorrow can also know great joy because of the depths they have experienced. Growth from traumatic or painful experiences has been shown to result in more personal strength, greater appreciation, deeper relationships, discovering new meaning in life, and seeing new possibilities. But if you're in the middle of the storm now, this can be cold comfort. You could try to think of ways this will make you stronger in the end. Or, try asking yourself what you need to do now to make it so. Ask: What do I need to do to make this something I can grow through? Perhaps you need to seek help healing. Perhaps you need to focus on yourself. Perhaps you need to get back up to the helm and steer the ship. There *is* a sunrise on the horizon. Set your course.

# Be Humble, Not Perfect

Hope is not about perfection. Perfection doesn't exist. Chasing it will only make you feel helpless, as if you are grasping for wind that your fingers can't hold no matter how hard you try. You will make mistakes on this journey. Don't be afraid. Living in hope requires you to take risks. You need to imagine new possibilities, things that have never been, and things that could be different than they are now. There is inherent risk in this as there is uncertainty. Find ways to let go of perfectionism by taking calculated risks and embracing the inevitable mistakes you'll make along the way. They're all steps of hope guiding you if you learn from them with humility. Ask for honest feedback from someone you admire. Turn to a coach who will help you improve. Be humble in what you do. And return to this mantra when the pain of failure stings you: "Failure is not final—it's a fulcrum." A fulcrum is like a lever. Use your failures as motivation to keep trying something new. The only real way to fail is if you don't try. Your effort is enough.

Life is a series of natural and spontaneous changes. Don't resist them—that only creates sorrow. Let reality be reality. Let things flow naturally forward in whatever way they like.

—LAO TZU
*Chinese philosopher*

# Do No Harm

Not everyone is aware of this, but the practice of yoga offers more than the physical exercises and shapes that you associate with the practice. Yoga is about mindfulness and meditation and also includes philosophic principles for life. One of the eight limbs of yoga is called *ahimsa* in Sanskrit. It's a principle found in several religions as well that means "non-harm." It's a great foundation for hope because it doesn't just mean not harming other beings—it starts with not harming yourself. It's a simple (though that's not to say easy!) practice to return to when things seem out of your control and you need to feel positive in how you show up in the world.

Consider *ahimsa* in what you think, what you say, and what you do. At the end of the day, reflect on your thoughts, words, and actions and ask yourself where you showed *ahimsa* and where you need to continue to practice it.

# Feel Held and Secure

When you've been through a lot, you might have a perpetual feeling of being unsafe. You might cope by feeling somewhat detached from the world around you and even from your own body. Hope is about safety rather than fear. To come back to a feeling of being secure and safe, try a weighted blanket. Lying under a weighted blanket might help your body feel calm and held, which can translate to your mind feeling comforted as well. There are specialized blankets for this that you can buy, but you can also experiment with laying a heavy pillow or yoga bolster across your hips or over your torso. Set a timer for ten minutes and lie down under the weight. Relax your breathing. Scan your body from your toes to your head, noticing how the weight feels at every point of contact and consciously releasing any held tension you have. Notice how it feels to be protected and wrapped up securely.

# Be Okay with Not Being Okay

Your impulse when things are not okay might be to "fix" what's wrong. Do you sometimes feel like you won't be okay until something is better or different? Maybe you think you'll be okay when you lose the weight. Maybe you're waiting to feel okay when you're more financially secure. Maybe you feel you need a partner to be okay with yourself. This is a kind of resistance to how you feel in the moment. It's okay to feel the pain, the fear, the grief. It's okay to feel not strong enough sometimes. It's okay to lack the willpower you want to have. These are natural experiences and, unfortunately, the only way out is through. Honor what you feel, but know it is also impermanent. Work with the feeling rather than against it. Consider a different perspective to the idea that you'll be okay when this thing is "fixed." What if it won't be different or "fixed" until you are first okay? Practice radical acceptance first and you might find that the grip of what bothers you weakens as a result. Be okay with not being okay, using this mantra: "I accept myself, just as I am now."

✦

# Life's like a movie, write your own ending. Keep believing, keep pretending.

—JIM HENSON
*American puppeteer and filmmaker*

# Open a New Chapter

When things fall apart, it's natural to experience a crisis of hope. Everything you believed in and thought to be true is crumbling around you. The cracking open of your understanding is deeply painful. What was working for you, the values you held, the future you dreamed of, might now feel inadequate, wrong, or impossible. You know you can't go back because you've been changed. You're not sure what comes after this. You might mourn the person you were before this experience broke you open. You have a choice at these moments. And it's an incredibly important one because when you're at your lowest you are also at your most vulnerable to whatever might enter the temporary void. What you thought you knew has failed you and you're struggling to see what could possibly come next. Your choice now is whether to let this be your story or whether to open a new chapter. At this pivotal moment, choose hope. Turn the page.

# Ask for Someone's Story

Everyone has a story. Individual stories weave in and out of each other creating a collective narrative like an intricate tapestry that you won't see unless you step back once in a while to admire it. You're part of these narratives, connected by threads of memories and language that give shape to your time in this world. This carries so much hope because you are never merely an island—you are part of the unending drama full of love, promise, and potential. Listening to the stories you're connected to brings expansion, compassion, and empathy.

Ask someone in your family about their story. Sit down over a leisurely cup of coffee. Ask about the time in their life that was most meaningful to them. Ask them to tell you about a moment that shaped who they became. Ask about a time where things changed and they were never the same. Ask for a story about what they rebelled against as a teenager. Ask to hear about their first love. Ask what they miss the most. Ask about their regrets. There's a good chance you'll be surprised at what you learn. Listen openly. Understand how you fit into this wider story that is still unfolding.

# Stay True to Your Values

What do your actions say about what you value? Your values are what you live to. They represent your most important beliefs. But have you spent much time digging deep into what they are? You might value hope, but find yourself acting out of pessimism and feeling despair. How you choose to act often makes some sense even when it doesn't seem like it at first. This is in part because what you want to *think* you value isn't necessarily what you *do* value. Consider being healthy. Most people say they want to be fit and have energy. And yet given the chance, these same people might indulge in junk food and buy a gym membership but never go. What gives? A higher value is driving the behavior. Perhaps the higher value is feeling good. You can value things that don't do you any favors if you don't stop to think about them. You could have learned negative values because of how you were treated in the past and developed ways of responding that served you then, but fail you now. Take some time to identify what's important so that you can stay true to the values that align you in hope.

1. Write out your top five values.
2. Write about a specific time you felt aligned with each of these values.
3. Now write about a specific time where you felt out of alignment with these values.
4. Can you identify what the underlying value was that took you out of alignment with where you want to be? Can you find strategies to elevate the top values that are important to you?

✦

# Begin at once to live, and count each separate day as a separate life.

—SENECA
*Roman philosopher*

# Greet the Messengers

There's no "right" or "wrong" way to feel. Emotions evolved to get your attention and influence you to act. They're often responses that you can't control. Your feelings are usually in the driver's seat, no matter how logical you think you are or how much willpower you try to develop. Studies have found that far from being a distraction or something to master with rational thinking, emotions are crucial to decision making. They point you in a direction. They have something to tell you. This is not to say that your emotions always serve you, however. It takes some practice to figure out what your emotions are trying to say and in what ways you want to listen to them. Emotional regulation is like a conversation between your feelings and your thinking mind. They might not be used to talking to each other. Try this exercise to sit them down at the table.

1. Ask: What triggered the strong emotion you're feeling right now?
2. Ask: What story are you telling yourself about this emotion? Are you justifying the feeling, and is it completely calling the shots? Are you denying the feeling and pushing it down and rationalizing?
3. Work with your feelings, not against them. See the emotion clearly. What are the facts? What do you know to be true?
4. What is this emotion telling you? Honor what you feel. Then decide what you want to do about it.

# Write Yourself a Love Letter

Are you your harshest critic? Perhaps the patience, understanding, and love you extend to others doesn't flow as easily in your own direction. While it's good to be humble and not have an over-inflated ego, it's equally important to be kind to yourself, especially when things are difficult or going wrong in your life and you need to find hope.

Write a love letter to yourself. Tell yourself what you appreciate about yourself, in the same way as if you were writing to a lover or close friend who needed a pick-me-up. Think about things you're proud of, challenges you've overcome, and contributions you've made, however small they might feel to you. Interrogate any feelings of unworthiness that might come up as you start to list what's so great about you. Where do these feelings come from? What would it feel like to acknowledge what makes you so great? Thank yourself for showing up for yourself. Give yourself some validation. Sign your letter with an affirmation that you are good and worthy of love, just as you are. Tuck this letter into a drawer near your bedside and read it whenever you need the reminder.

# Take Yourself on a Date

In the routines of daily life—the nine-to-five, the school pick-up, the meal-planning, sports night, volunteering, dinner with friends, paying the bills, and just plain old living—you might not take much time to be with just yourself. It might even feel more comfortable to actively avoid alone time altogether. Do you fill every silence with noise? Maybe the second you're alone in the car you put on music or a podcast. Perhaps you take any downtime and make it productive through learning or doing chores or just always being busy, busy, busy.

When was the last time you left the phone at home and took yourself out, just to be in your own company? Try it. Go to the park or a cafe. Visit a museum or go to the movies by yourself. People watch. Take in your surroundings. Notice where your mind wanders when you're alone and there is nothing to stimulate you and distract you from yourself and whatever you're experiencing in the moment. It might be very uncomfortable or even painful at first. There might be a reason you've been avoiding yourself that you need to take the time to see. But it might be that confronting this will help to unlock your mind into a greater sense of peace with yourself and generate ideas for you that kindle a new hope within, free from distraction and avoidance. Embrace your solitude. Disconnect for a moment so that you may reconnect with greater energy.

✦

I have discovered
in life that there
are ways of getting
almost anywhere
you want to go, if you
really want to go.

—LANGSTON HUGHES
*American poet, writer, and activist*

# Get Off the Couch

Dreaming of something grand for your future can be exciting. It can also be paralyzing. The problem comes when you hyper-focus on a specific outcome. You might think you'll only be happy when you arrive at this destination. And at the same time, the endpoint feels so far away. You lose sight of the joy in the journey itself and never get started. The thing is, even if you achieve your goal, the good feeling you get from it will be temporary. Focus on your efforts, not the outcomes.

Learning to run when you've never run before is a great way to develop this mindset. This couch-to-5k program breaks down a big goal of running 5 kilometers and focuses on the process of getting there. Here are weekly steps for a slightly modified version of the program. Each step should be done three times in that week. For every run, begin with a five-minute brisk walk.

1. Run for sixty seconds and walk for ninety seconds, alternating this for a total of fifteen minutes.
2. Run for ninety seconds and walk for two minutes for over fifteen minutes.
3. Work up to three minutes of walking and three minutes of running for over fifteen minutes.
4. Work up to five minutes of running into your fifteen-minute sessions.
5. Work up to running for twenty minutes over your three runs this week.
6. Run for twenty-five minutes straight.
7. Run for twenty-eight minutes straight.
8. Run for thirty minutes straight.

# Write a Poem

Poetry is delightful, surprising, and unexpected wordplay that conveys a lot of meaning in an often abstract way. There are forms of poetry you can study, but prose poetry is simply about working to a rhythm you can define for yourself. Don't worry about the rulebook. You don't have to rhyme or study sonnets for this. Try these poem prompts to focus on expressing something you feel.

- Tell your life story in exactly six lines.
- Write a letter to your hopes.
- Start with this line: "Things I have learned…"
- Write a poem about the last photo you took.
- Think of an experience, whether positive or negative, and write how you felt, not what actually happened.
- Turn one of the last texts you sent into the start of a poem.
- Take a line from a poem you love as a starting line and remix it into something new.
- Create an "erasure" poem by finding a print article and blacking out all the words you don't want to use. You'll be creating sentences by leaving choice words uncovered in the text.
- Create a poem about a dream you've had.

# Breathe with a Lion's Power

If it's intense worry and anxiety building in you that is keeping you from a more hopeful outlook, try this little breathing exercise. Lion breathing is like a release valve for intense, hard-to-handle emotions.

1. Sit comfortably and bring your awareness to your natural breath. Notice if it's tight and constricted in your chest and where the breath moves in your body.
2. Take a deep breath through your nose.
3. As you breathe out, open your mouth, stick your tongue out as if you were a big cat, and sigh out your exhale loudly.
4. Repeat and make your sigh even louder. Don't be shy—let it out! With this exhale, let out any of the anxiety or tension you feel along with it.
5. Repeat for at least five complete rounds of breath until you feel calmer and less gripped by what you were feeling at the start.
6. Notice how you feel now as you return to your natural breath's rhythm.

✦

One child, one
teacher, one
book, one pen can
change the world.

—MALALA YOUSAFZAI
*Pakistani activist*

# Experiment with a Sculpture

Boosting your creative skills and your ways of approaching a problem can boost your resiliency skills as well. This is a fun way to get out of your head and to think about the idea of support as you try to balance a marshmallow using spaghetti. Try it with a friend or in a group and see what kinds of solutions you can come up with. For this one, read step one and don't read step two until you've completed step one.

1. Take a handful of uncooked spaghetti and a large marshmallow. Set a timer for up to twenty minutes. In that time, use the spaghetti to build the tallest structure you can that will support a marshmallow on top of it.
2. Reflect on your approach. How much time did you spend thinking and planning? How much time did you spend experimenting? And how much time did you spend building?

What this exercise sometimes shows is that adults tend to plan and build one thing, whereas children experiment and try little concepts before building up to bigger ones. It's an adult tendency to want to plan in order to control the outcome, but when you allow yourself the freedom to experiment, that's where the magic happens. Can you make more room in your life for trying new things in new ways?

# Find a Mentor

Another great way to build connection—one of the key factors of resilience—is to find a teacher or mentor. Learning is a lifelong endeavor, not something that ends when you graduate. Mastery is a lifelong process, not a destination you arrive at. You can learn different things from different people in your life. Consider this approach developed by a martial arts teacher and apply it to whatever it is you are most passionate about learning in life.

1. Find someone who is more advanced than you. This mentor can teach you what you don't know yet. It can be difficult to know what you don't know. This person will help you level up.
2. Find someone who is on the same level as you. This person is someone you can challenge yourself against, who will motivate you to do better.
3. Find someone who isn't as advanced as you. This is someone who you can teach what you know. When you teach someone else, you solidify your own skills and knowledge and you continue to push yourself through assessing your own skills.

# Make Room for Play

Play comes naturally to children. There's an uninhibited curiosity with which kids charge at life and it holds so much imagination and positivity. Play is the opposite of trauma. It's healing. But as adults, it can seem silly to indulge in play for the sake of play. See how it feels to let yourself go in some childlike pursuits.

- Play in the rain. Jump in puddles. Get messy in the mud.
- Jump on a trampoline. Really go for it. Close your eyes, swing your arms, get higher and higher.
- Swing on the swings at a park. Kick your legs to get as high as you can before jumping off. Sit and twist up the chain before releasing it and letting it go, twirling and getting dizzy.
- Build a blanket fort. Gather all the pillows and blankets you have, drape them over chairs and couches. Retreat into a comfy maze of tunnels and relax in the dim light of the cave you've created.
- Finger paint. Squish the pigment between your hands and move intuitively to draw color over the page.

◆

# Life can only be understood backward; but it must be lived forward.

—SØREN KIERKEGAARD
*Danish philosopher and theologian*

# Fill Your Home with Pleasing Scents

Your sense of smell can be a subtle yet powerful one to tap into to create a calming environment and an anchor to feeling hopeful. Smell is closely tied to memory. Consider what smells transport you to a peaceful time where you felt secure and safe in exploring the possibilities before you. Fill your entire house with this scent and notice how it makes you feel. Here are some suggestions.

- Light a scented candle.
- Bake a loaf of bread or some cookies. There's a reason that realtors holding open houses use this tactic—it's comforting and homey!
- Buy a bouquet of flowers.
- Try an aromatherapy diffuser. Experiment with different scents based on the feeling you want to evoke.
- Make use of essential oils. Try lavender on your pillow before you go to sleep or in an eye mask that you can relax with.

# Draw Something to See Clearly

You might assume you see with your eyes. However, in a way, you're processing a lot of information through your senses and at the same time your brain is taking a lot of shortcuts. When things become routine and familiar, you aren't necessarily seeing the things you're looking at. Bring back a sense of wonder, possibility, and creativity through this drawing technique. You don't have to know how to draw! You don't have to create something you'd put in a gallery. You just have to move your pencil on a piece of paper and loosen up.

1. Take an object and give yourself sixty seconds to draw it.
2. Turn your subject to a new angle and give yourself two minutes on it.
3. Turn it again and give yourself five minutes of drawing time.
4. Once again, turn your object to a new angle and draw what you see for fifteen minutes.
5. Take a moment to reflect on the difference you felt progressing through these timeframes. Could you loosen up when you had such little time to worry about being perfect or good? How did the timeframe and focus on a single object change what you saw and captured? Were you able to focus more on the details when you took the time to really see it?

# Set Your Boundaries

Have you ever found yourself in a situation where you compromise your own hopes for someone else? This isn't about a healthy compromise within a relationship, but about those times where you felt in your gut that you didn't like what was happening, but you compromised yourself and accepted it anyway. Having a healthy understanding of your boundaries—what it is you're willing to accept in how others treat you—is fundamental to realizing your own dreams. Reflect on these writing prompts to build—and enforce—stronger boundaries.

1. Think of a situation where you were uncomfortable with how you were treated by someone over a period of time. It's time to get honest. List out the red flags you saw and ignored. These are the times your gut was saying it wasn't right, but you looked past it. These are boundaries being crossed that you ignored.

2. Look at these items and, with understanding and compassion for yourself, consider what it would mean to look at yourself through the prism of how you were treated. For example, this list would say that this person feels they're not worthy of respect, or love, or consideration. What would you say if it was your best friend being treated this way?

3. Now, list out how you want to be treated. Notice the differences here between this list and what you might have accepted in the past.

4. Create a plan for what you'll do in the future when your boundaries are crossed. Take your power back. Don't compromise your own hopes and dreams for poor treatment.

✦

# If you don't set your own agenda, somebody else will.

—MELINDA GATES
*American philanthropist*

# Create a Battle Plan

Hope is taking action despite your fears. Knowing what you want, believing it is possible, and going for it, is how you live in hope. This is so much easier said than done! You will find all the excuses in the book as your doubts surface. Consider the cost of inaction with this thought exercise based on an idea from author Tim Ferriss.

1. Define a dream or something you really want to do but are afraid to start by completing the sentence: *What if I....* What if I wrote that book? What if I quit my job? What if I married that person? What if I started a family? What if I traveled for a year? What if I started that business?
2. Looking at your "what if," define the worst-case scenario. In what ways are you going to fail at this? How will that impact your life?
3. Write down how you can prevent that worst-case scenario. Who could you rely on to help? What plan could you put in place to give yourself the greatest shot at this?
4. Now consider how you could repair the situation if the worst-case scenario came to pass. What could you do to pivot or rebuild or keep going?
5. Imagine what it would be like to succeed. What does success at this look like? What if you even managed to get halfway there?
6. If you do nothing toward this dream, what will this cost you? Will it matter in six months? Twelve months? Five years? What impact will it have on your life, whether it be emotionally, physically, or financially? Can you afford *inaction*?

# Don't Let Hope Wither

Treat hope like a verb rather than a noun. Your hope isn't something you merely *have*—it's something you *do*. And action requires you to make a decision on what you want for your life and your future. The poet Sylvia Plath tells a story of someone sitting under a fig tree. Each fig is ripe and juicy and represents different choices, such as whether to get married and start a family, whether to become a writer, or whether to travel. Each choice has a trade-off. In other words, she can't eat all the figs at once. But as she sits under the tree, unable to decide which one to take, the figs turn overripe. They fall to the ground, where they begin to rot. It's a powerful metaphor for your hopes and dreams. Without action, they remain on the vine, until it becomes too late to do any of them.

Think of everything you hope to do in life. What action are you taking toward these goals? Are you paralyzed by indecision and not doing anything at all? It's comfortable to plan and think and watch all of these hopes and dreams blossoming as beautiful ideas on the tree. But to get anything moving, you need to decide. You need to choose what action to take.

# Develop Relationships That Inspire You

They say that you are the average of the five people you spend the most time with. Look around you at your close circle of friends and family. Does it include people you admire and want to be like? Are they positive and supportive by nature? Or are they negative and always tearing you down rather than adding any light to your life?

Psychotherapist Ken Page talks about relationships as consisting primarily of either deprivation or inspiration. Consider how you feel and your energy when you're around the people you're close to. Are they giving you energy or taking it from you? Do they inspire you or make you feel small? No relationship is inspirational all the time. There are times of give and take. But, on balance, if a relationship doesn't feel good to you, it might be time to ask what purpose it serves in your life. Watch out for relationships where you feel you need to *earn* the love or respect of the other person. Surround yourself with the kind of hopeful people you want to become. Be generous with these people. Give and receive inspiration in your relationships.

◆

Other people's views and troubles can be contagious. Don't sabotage yourself by unwittingly adopting negative, unproductive attitudes through your associations with others.

—EPICTETUS
*Greek philosopher*

# Tell Someone How You Feel

Feeling lonely is its own crisis of hope. On the flip side, strong relationships are a formidable source of hope. Take some time to develop and deepen a relationship by expressing what you feel to someone in your life. Include both the positive and negative! Don't keep your feelings to yourself. Expressing what you feel is an act of vulnerability. It takes courage because it raises the stakes. You're opening up and you won't know how it will be received. Trust and communicate effectively. Try these conversation starters to help express what you feel.

- I feel _____ because _____.
- When _____ happened, I felt _____.
- When you do _____ I feel _____. I really need _____ instead.
- I need to feel _____.

You still can't control whether you'll be heard or understood. But you'll have communicated something meaningful in a way that opens up a door rather than blames or causes friction between you. Listen to the response you receive. See how it feels to be open with what you feel, even when it's difficult.

# Develop Loving-Kindness

Hope is, in many ways, a neutral concept, meaning it can be positive or negative. You might automatically assume all hope is positive. But if what you hope for is clouded by bitterness, it's far from a positive force. You might be enviously wishing for someone to get what you think they deserve or silently hoping they'll fail. Consider this hope as less about the other person and a sense of what's right and fair, and more about something within *you* that you need to confront. Use these negative hopes as a mirror to look at yourself, your ego, and your own insecurities. Counter these negativities with compassion using this loving-kindness meditation.

1. Set a timer for five to ten minutes.
2. Close your eyes as you sit down in a comfortable way for meditation.
3. Begin by noticing your breath, breathing in and out from your nose.
4. Think of someone you are struggling with, toward whom you have caught yourself having negative thoughts.
5. Holding this person in your mind, say to them: "May you be happy. May you be healthy and strong. May you be peaceful."
6. Continue to hold this person and this wish for them in your mind until your timer goes. Notice how you feel afterward and whether you can release the grip of insecurity or bitterness that ties you to envious and judgmental feelings.

# Collect and Give Good Wishes

It's not often that you might tell the people in your life what they mean to you in all the little day-to-day ways. Try this one with your family, a group of friends, or even your coworkers to capture and share on a regular basis.

1. Create an envelope with a piece of paper. It doesn't have to be folded in any fancy way. You're creating a pocket that slips of paper can be stuck into.
2. Decorate your envelope with your name and any embellishments you like. Have some fun with it and be expressive with some color, paint, glitter, or whatever you have to hand.
3. Hang your envelope with your group. This could be in your living room if it's for your family, in the lunchroom at work, or in a room you and your friends often gather. Hang the envelopes on a string like bunting, stick them with a magnet to the fridge, or create a letter tree like a kind of Christmas tree, clipping them to a frame.
4. Over the course of a month, everyone in the group is to write down on a small scrap of paper anytime they appreciate a person, want to thank them, or want to express how they feel about that person and place it in that person's envelope.
5. At the end of the month, everyone can take their envelope. Rather than opening it and reading all of your messages, save it somewhere and draw one piece of paper when you're in need of a boost of hope.

◆

It is not true
that people stop
pursuing dreams
because they grow
old, they grow old
because they stop
pursuing dreams.

—GABRIEL GARCÍA MÁRQUEZ
*Colombian novelist and journalist*

# Deal with Rejection and Setbacks

Not getting what you desire could be a blow to your hope and optimism. Whether it's a promotion you've been denied, a love interest who isn't interested, or a project flop, rejection stings. It's natural to feel hurt and to want to protect yourself. Here are some tips to channel a setback into a positive course that will keep you on the road to hope.

- Acknowledge how you feel with honesty. Tell yourself you understand how you feel and it makes sense given the situation.
- Separate the rejection or criticism or setback from your personal identity. Someone else not liking something you've done or who you are can say more about that person than you. View negative feedback as related to things you can learn about your work or your efforts, not as critical of *you* and your worth as a human being.
- Be persistent. "No" is never a final answer if you use it as motivation to learn, improve, and try again in a different way. Work to understand why you are being told no so that you can turn it into a "yes."

# Wash Away an Intense Emotion

Certain emotions can be so intense that they take you over. Anger, grief, despair—when you're under these emotions sometimes it takes more than simply being hopeful to pull yourself out. Sometimes you might even find that the emotion itself is a reaction to a deeper pain, fear, or hurt that has been triggered. Try naming, honoring, and releasing what you feel with this little exercise.

1. Get some chalk and find a space outside that you can draw on that is quiet and private.
2. Write down what you're feeling. Make the letters as big as the emotion feels within you.
3. Look at what you've written. Think for a moment about what caused this feeling.
4. Notice how you feel in your body. How does the feeling show up? Are there any areas of tension, perhaps in your jaw or behind your eyes? Are you clenching or holding anywhere?
5. Wash away what you've written. Throw a bucket of water across it.
6. As you watch the colors mix and mingle and wash away, notice if the feeling within you and your body is diminishing in its power too.

# Gaze at a Partner

Hope is a vulnerable exercise because it means wanting to change or improve things and there is no guarantee you can make this happen. Sometimes it seems as though modern culture views vulnerability as a weakness only, as if it is something to harden yourself against. It makes sense because to be vulnerable is to be open to pain and you would be wise to try to avoid pain if you can. But when you harden rather than open, you close yourself off to the good stuff in life too. Vulnerability is a risk, but, like all great risks, there can be great rewards. Practice this skill through a gazing meditation with a partner.

1. Sit across from your partner in a comfortable position.
2. Set a timer for ten minutes.
3. Rather than staring intensely into the other person's eyes, let your gazes be relaxed and soft as you look at each other. It might help you to look into one of their eyes or between their eyes.
4. Acknowledge to each other if this feels weird or silly or uncomfortable. You might both be feeling the same thing and naming it can bring greater understanding and bring you closer together.
5. When the timer goes, talk to each other about this experience. How did you feel during it? How do you feel now? Notice if your sense of intimacy is increased by this vulnerable experiencing of looking and being looked at.

✦

It is important to expect nothing, to take every experience, including the negative ones, as merely steps on the path, and to proceed.

—RAM DASS

*American spiritual teacher, psychologist, and author*

# Seek Someone Who Will Understand

Few things will be more alienating to you and your sense of hope than being misunderstood or disconnected from other people. It's true what they say—it is usually better to be alone than to feel you are alone because you are with the wrong person. The need for connection is a core evolutionary drive. It's important to make sure the connections you spend time on are high-quality ones, especially when you need to build a hopeful outlook. Remember that it's about depth and quality, not quantity. A small handful of people you can count on, who build you up rather than tear you down, are worth the world. Try this journaling exercise to appreciate the ones who understand you.

Write about three moments in your life where you experienced deep vulnerability and intimacy with someone else and where you felt safe to do so. Be specific in recalling times where you were understood or moved by them and recall in detail what that felt like. Think of the people in your life who it feels easy to be around and with whom you can let your guard down. Who can you rely on no matter what? Who makes you feel more energized after spending time with them rather than depleted? Consciously commit to investing in your core people with openness and honesty. You could start by telling them what you appreciate about them through the moments you've written about—this act itself can open up space for greater vulnerability as it's not often people take the opportunity to do this in the day-to-day.

# Do Less of What You Dislike

Figuring out what you want out of life can be your entire life's project. Finding purpose seems to come naturally to some and is a more difficult road for others. Without this deeper sense of meaning, you might lose hope. If you're searching for what you're meant to be doing with this one crazy and beautiful life you have, start with the opposite: what you don't want. In some ways, it can be easier to identify what you don't like than what lights you up. Starting to eliminate the options might point you toward what makes you feel more fulfilled. On a sheet of paper, complete the following sentences.

- I feel most unhappy when I _____.
- I can't imagine doing _____ for the rest of my life.
- I'm good at _____ but hate doing it.
- I don't understand why anybody would _____.
- I dread whenever I have to _____.

Are there any surprises here? What do you notice about what you don't want for your life and how you're living now? Is there any action you can take now to start moving away from what you know you don't want? You don't have to know what you're moving toward yet. Trust that it's still the right direction if you're leaving behind what doesn't move you.

# Make a Jar of Hope

Although hope is about the future, it's important not to live for some imagined ideal time because this will rob you of your present experiences. What can you do today to connect to hope? Create a jar of hope that you can draw on whenever you need a reminder of what you already have and what you're excited to see unfolding.

1. Clean an old glass jam or sauce jar. Remove the label.
2. Decorate your jar so that it's something you'll smile at when you see it. You could paint your name on it. You could label it "hopes and dreams." You could paint a rainbow or starry sky.
3. On small slips of paper, write down things you are grateful for, things you hope for, and quotes that ground or inspire you. Stick these in your jar and keep adding to them whenever a thought occurs to you that should be included.
4. Whenever you find yourself down about your present moment, draw on a slip of paper. Notice how it makes you feel.
5. On New Year's Eve, plan to empty your jar and reflect on the year that has just gone and the fresh one before you. Is there anything no longer relevant? Take stock of the progress you've made in a year and what you want to do with the new one.

✦

# Life changes in the instant. The ordinary instant.

—JOAN DIDION
*American writer*

# Ask Someone How They Are

What do you say when someone asks you: "How are you?" Most of us have a ready response. "Fine, thanks, and you?" "Okay." "Can't complain." It's a cultural greeting, a call and response, that is largely automatic. Let's be honest—these automatic responses never get to the heart of the question. This becomes apparent when you or someone you know is facing a great difficulty. You've probably experienced it, where someone asks how you are and you might want to scream, "How do you *think*?" Or, you might not know what to say to someone else when you know what they're facing and they can't be comforted by words. When you are in pain, or when you know others are, there is still a great need to feel connected and supported. Pretending nothing is wrong or avoiding the issue with silence doesn't help.

What would it be like if you could use this question as an opener for true vulnerability? It's an opportunity to draw on support that can buoy you during difficult times. Open space for someone to talk by asking, "How are you *today*?" Don't worry about saying the right or wrong thing. Simply ask, genuinely, in a way that acknowledges this isn't just the usual greeting. Your opening won't necessarily be accepted. But still, offer it. On the other side, respond to someone asking how you are with your own vulnerability. Acknowledge they might not know what to say, but listening might help. This space offered for someone to talk about what they're going through or how they feel is one of the greatest gifts of love.

# Curate the Noise

There's no denying it: This is an information age. News and information are so constant that it can be overwhelming. When you're surrounded by noise all the time, you miss the signal. Think of it like an alarm. A smoke alarm is usually a rare sound to hear and a signal to evacuate. But a car alarm that constantly goes off becomes background noise and no one goes to investigate because everyone assumes it's a false alarm. You can miss the important signals that require your attention when you are awash in noise. Negative noise crowds out signals of hope. Try these digital minimalism tips to reduce the noise in your life. Intentionally choose what you give your attention to so that you don't miss the positive signals.

- Remove any apps on your phone that you haven't used in the past three months.
- Turn off notifications except for important people. Silence messages and choose when you look at them and respond, rather than being pulled away by every buzz or ding.
- Notice how you feel when scrolling social media. Are you uplifted or envious? Curated lives are not a good picture of reality. Cut out channels that make you feel negative. Unfollow or silence people and brands that don't make you feel good.
- Schedule device downtime, for example in the evening after dinner. Turn your phone off for an hour or two and put it in a drawer out of sight.

These exercises might cause anxiety at first. Try it over time and notice how it feels to be free of so much unnecessary noise.

# Take Action; Don't Wait for Motivation

Hope without action is passive, and passive hope is not likely to take you very far. If you're waiting for motivation to strike in order to pursue your dreams, you will be waiting a long time. The truth is, no amount of simply sending out wishes will get you what you want if you're not willing to recognize the opportunities when they come and take action. What you'll find when you do is that action leads to feeling motivated, not the other way around. Act before you feel like it and it will be like a snowball running downhill, getting larger and larger, gaining momentum all its own. When you really don't feel like it, try breaking it down with this Pomodoro method—a twenty-five-minute exercise that can help get you going.

1. Shut off your phone, close your email, and remove any distractions.
2. Set a timer for twenty-five minutes.
3. For the next twenty-five minutes, focus on a task. Because it's such a short time, you can commit to this. You don't have to complete anything, you only have to start. Break down the next steps on what it is you want to do and get going.
4. When the timer goes, notice how you feel. Maybe you want to keep going. Maybe you want to take a five-minute break and then do another twenty-five. Often starting is the hardest part. Get started and create momentum.

◆

# I've often lost myself, in order to find the burn that keeps everything awake.

—FEDERICO GARCÍA-LORCA
*Spanish poet and playwright*

# Embrace Your Solitude and Your Community

Loneliness is an enemy of hope. When you feel disconnected and alone, it's a fast road to hopelessness. Of course being alone is not the same as being lonely. But the fact is that humans are a connected species. Even our close relatives, the chimps, band together in difficulty. There is strength in numbers. Love your solitude for the opportunity it provides you to be with yourself, to listen, and to understand who you are. At the same time, do not deny your needs to be socially connected. Channel any loneliness into a drive to find and forge connections with yourself and with others. Find people who challenge you and make you a better person and offer the same gift to them. Create a virtuous circle of community and build hope together.

# Connect to a Higher Purpose

Resilience requires finding meaning in what you struggle with. At its heart, this is a project of feeling connected to a bigger picture, beyond yourself. When you stop to consider what it all means, it can seem like a scary and overwhelming question to ask. You might even wonder whether you truly have a purpose. Connecting to something larger than yourself is a good starting point to think about this question. For some people, it's their faith or spiritual beliefs. For others, it's nature, volunteering, or being creative. If you're struggling to find out what this might be for you, try this journaling exercise for one month.

Every day, write down what made you feel connected. Make this as specific as you can. Pay attention for moments where time seemed to fly by, where your interactions with people made you feel good, and where you felt joy. After thirty days, review what you've written and notice any patterns. Do you feel most connected when helping others? Working on something in-depth? Creating? Learning? Being physical? Being in nature or with animals? Ask yourself why you felt connected in the moments you've written down. Think of ways you can bring in more of these connecting moments to your life to reduce the disconnection. Over time, your purpose might become more clear. Don't stress if you struggle to find a clear purpose statement for yourself now. It's your entire life's work to explore, to give, and to grow into it.

✦

You may not control
all the events that
happen to you, but
you can decide not to
be reduced by them.

—MAYA ANGELOU
*American poet and activist*

# Sit Beside Water

Like the practice of forest bathing, sitting beside a body of water is a very effective way to connect with nature that can bring calm to your mind. Water is a source of life and, perhaps as a result, seems to have hopeful properties. Head to a water source close to you and spend an hour or two mindfully watching it. Notice the waves, whether they are large saltwater ocean crests, river eddies, or small laps on a lakeside shore. Attune to this rhythm and how similar to breathing it is. Notice how it flows, perhaps fast or gentle on a river or calm and still on a pond. Observe the wildlife that comes here for sustenance. The birds that dive for fish or vegetation. The insects that disturb flat surfaces with little rings that echo outward. The seaweed, lilies, and bulrushes that grow up around the edges. Watch the reflection of clouds, cliffs, and trees. Wherever you are, take this moment to feel how the water connects you to everything on this tiny blue dot of a planet.

# Talk to the Pros

In what ways do you make sure you take care of your body? And in what ways do you take the time to care for your mind? Many think nothing of joining a gym or hiring a personal trainer, but looking for a therapist can still seem to be something only for when things are going very wrong or you're diagnosed with an illness. Thankfully, the idea of therapy has become much less stigmatized in recent years. But if you think that it's only for when you have big problems, think again. Consider taking care of your mental health as you would your physical health to show yourself care anytime, no matter what is going on in your life.

Positive psychology is the art of living well. Having space from someone impartial and nonjudgmental to talk through what you think and feel can help give you perspective and new ways of seeing old patterns. Many therapists offer free consultations, and it's important to find someone with whom you feel comfortable to get the most out of it. Increasingly, online services are also now available, and virtual therapy can be just as effective as it is in-person, so you can find a way to work it into your schedule. Try it and you might be surprised.

# Dress Up for No Reason

Self-care might seem like something to indulge in when you need a pick-me-up. It will serve you better, however, if it's built into your daily life like maintenance. You don't take your car to the shop after the engine has blown up. You take it in for a check, an oil change, and a tune-up to prevent further problems down the line. But when things are going well in your life, it can be easy to slip into putting off your self-care. You might find yourself hitting a low point and without the energy to get back to it. It's more important than ever at these times to care for yourself. When you don't feel like it, don't put self-care off until tomorrow. Do something that makes you feel good and it will help.

One way to try this, to jolt yourself out of a funk, is to get dressed up for no reason. Take a long shower with all of your favorite products. Pamper your skin and make yourself smell amazing. Do whatever makes you feel confident. It could be putting on makeup or not putting on makeup. Style your hair and wear your favorite outfit. Even if you have nowhere to go, signal to yourself that you are worthy of this care. Notice how you feel showing this care to yourself just because.

✦

The "what should
be" never did exist,
but people keep
trying to live up to
it. There is no "what
should be," there is
only what is.

—LENNY BRUCE
*American comedian and satirist*

# Live to Your Own Standards

Are you avoiding pursuing your own hopes and dreams because you're always doing what you "should" be doing instead? Of course, there are the usual responsibilities of life and not everything you need to do is going to be exciting all the time. But those things still serve a larger goal or purpose for you. "Should" is based more in other people's expectations of you or your perception of what they think. Your avoidance could indicate there is something out of alignment with your authentic values. Drop the "shoulds" in your life by committing to living up to your own standards, not someone else's.

At the end of the day, journal about what you felt you should have done today, but didn't. Ask yourself why you didn't do it. Are you procrastinating? Are you afraid? Do you even want to do this thing or is guilt making you think you should? What would happen if you never got around to doing it? If you let go of it, how would it feel? What impact would it have on your life? You could also reflect more broadly on the day itself and write about the bigger things in life you feel you should be doing. See if writing these things out can help you to identify where you need to work toward your own goals and where you need to let go of things that are actually simply the expectations of others.

# Find a Way Around an Obstacle

Do you find yourself giving up when things get hard? When you encounter difficulty on the road to what you hope for, how do you respond? The obstacle in your path isn't the problem. In fact, it can even be seen as a gift. The obstacle, as author Ryan Holiday writes, is the way itself. The worst thing isn't what happens to you that pushes you off course. The problem arises when you lose your mind to what happens to you and allow it to block your path. A barrier may alter your path, but it's up to you whether it limits it. Focus on persistence and progress over perfection. Focus on what you can control—your effort, will, and the perspective you take—rather than external constraints. Hope lives in the action you take to get around any obstacles in your way.

# Ride the Wave

The only certainty in life is, perhaps ironically, that everything changes. This can make you wonder what your hopes are based on. You might even feel hopeless considering there is no destination to arrive at. Life is, after all, a perpetual struggle. Within this there is still a kind of hope found in the interconnectedness of everything. Reflect with this meditation based on an idea from Buddhist monk Thich Nhat Hanh.

1. Find a comfortable seat for meditation. Relax your gaze or close your eyes. Release any tension in your mind and body. Feel the breath move in you.
2. Picture yourself on a sandy beach by the ocean. Fill in the details of the clouds and the sky and the waves.
3. Now watch a single wave from a distance. Notice the shape of it and how it begins and ends in the wider sea. Watch it grow larger and crest before lapping onto the sands in front of where you stand.
4. Notice how the wave has disappeared. It existed and had its height and depth and movement and now it has dissolved back into the ocean water behind it. Its nature was always that it was part of the water, though for a short time it took the shape of the wave.
5. Reflect on what this means to you and the shape your life takes for the time you have it, before you blink your eyes open and return to the space where you sit.

◆

The most important words that have helped me in life, when things have gone right or when things have gone wrong, are "accept responsibility."

—BILLIE JEAN KING
*American professional tennis player*

# Forgive Someone

When someone has hurt you or wronged you, one of the hardest things you might ever do is forgive them. Yet it's also so necessary to set yourself free of the past and allow yourself to step into all you hope for in your future. Desmond Tutu, who served as the chairman of the Truth and Reconciliation Commission in South Africa, spoke about forgiveness as being "the best form of self-interest."

This is because when you hold on to anger and hatred for someone else, it keeps you chained to them. Don't feel shame for what you feel. As Tutu suggests, the depth of your anger at injustice shows the depth of your love. At the same time, don't let your anger consume you. Set yourself free through forgiveness. It's not about releasing the other person of responsibility, but about taking responsibility for yourself. What you most struggle to forgive is what you most need to let go. Try these steps from a Hawaiian tradition called ho'oponopono.

1. **APOLOGIZE.** Open the door to mutual forgiveness by saying "I'm sorry."
2. **FORGIVE.** Forgive the other person. Forgive yourself. Ask the other person for forgiveness too.
3. **LOVE.** Tell the person you love them as a fellow human being. Say to yourself that you love yourself.
4. **BE GRATEFUL.** Say thank you. Feel liberated and set free from what chained you to this person.

# Make a Bid of Connection

Your relationships will be a big influencer on how hopeful you feel. A long-running study by Harvard researchers has found that one of the biggest predictors of satisfaction with your life is the quality of your relationships. Take some time to check in on your most meaningful relationships using this way of looking at how you interact.

The Gottman Institute refers to bids of connections when it comes to building healthy relationships. A bid of connection is a bit like a call-and-response. It's reaching out, in however small of a way, to say "I'm here, do you see me?" It could be sharing something you found interesting or a gentle squeeze of a hand. What's important is the response you give and receive to the bids of connection in your relationships. You can turn away, ignoring the person's attempt at connecting with you. You can turn against them, snapping at them or shutting them down. Or, you can turn toward them, accepting the bid of connection and responding. Everyone has bad days and times they don't have as much to give. But in healthy relationships there are more responses of turning toward the other person.

Reflect on the key relationships in your life. What are the subtle ways you try to connect with others and how are these received? What are the ways others try to connect with you and how do you respond? If you find the responses tend to be on the negative side, consider it like a check engine light; it's time to look deeper at what is happening in the relationship.

# Offer to Help Someone Else

Hope is as much about yourself as it is about how you relate with others. If you feel lonely and in need of a friend, you could feel sorry for yourself and wonder why no one ever checks in or invites you to things. Or, you can become the friend you need. Pick up the phone and call someone to ask how they are these days. Invite someone to do something with you next week. You don't have to plan a big party or be an extrovert for this. Simply reach out to one person and let them know you're thinking of them. Ask them if they need anything. Make a coworker a cup of tea. Knock on your neighbor's door. In acting as a friend to someone else, you get a friend in return. You can draw emotional strength in supporting someone else and being someone who they can count on. This isn't to imply a transactional, tit-for-tat kind of relationship. What it means is that the act of being a friend can make you feel as good as having someone be a friend to you. It's true that it takes two—it just takes one to get it started sometimes.

✦

I like to wake up each morning and not know what I think, that I may reinvent myself in some way.

—STEPHEN FRY
*English actor and writer*

# Greet the Day with Hope

How do you wake up on a Monday morning? With dread? Or with hope? If you have more days than not of feeling as though a day is just something to get through rather than something to enjoy, it's time to consider why this is. Life is more about adding up your average Wednesdays than the exciting getaways you might take once a year.

Many skills in this book will serve you well in helping you build a resilient and hopeful mindset. Mindfulness helps you to see how your thought patterns influence how you see the world and your experiences. Changing your mind can change your life. Emotional regulation can help you to respond rather than react to life's stresses. Body awareness can help you process places you're stuck and bring you into mind-body alignment. Connection can help you find meaning and purpose. But your external reality is still something you need to face. If you're being ground down in an abusive situation, with soul-destroying work, or struggling with mental or physical problems, it might be time to go to the root cause and fiercely address the situation. What would it take to wake up with excitement for everything you get to do today?

# Borrow a Puppy

When you lose hope in your fellow human beings, it might help to spend some time with animals. If you don't have a pet of your own, you can still access this experience of unconditional love and comfort that seems to come naturally to some animals. Offer to walk a neighbor's dog or make use of one of the online services that enable you to borrow someone else's pet for the day. Cat sit for a friend on holiday or join a cat sitting volunteer service. You can reach out to local shelters or vets and ask about volunteer opportunities that involve a chance to spend time with the animals in their care. Remember that if you decide to get a pet of your own that this is a big responsibility and shouldn't be undertaken lightly. Consider fostering a cat or dog with a local rescue to see if it's for you. Whatever your experience, give and receive the affection of this innocent and loving creature and notice if it helps to fill your cup of unconditional hope too.

✦

# Do the thing you fear and the death of fear is certain.

—RALPH WALDO EMERSON
*American philosopher and poet*

# Build a Support Base

There is vulnerability in relying on others. At the same time, what you can create with the support of someone else or what you can enable in someone else by supporting them is so much greater than what you can do alone. Try this partner yoga exercise with someone to feel physically supported, and take that feeling with you as you take the risks you need to in order to forge strong, supportive relationships in your life.

1. Have a partner take Child's Pose by sitting back on their heels with knees wide and big toes touching. This person will fold forward and round their spine, resting their forehead on the ground and crawling their arms out in front of them.
2. The second person will then face away from the partner and, facing up to the ceiling, will gently roll their spine backward over the curved spine of the partner starting from their lower back. Try this with legs stretched out straight or knees bent and feet on the ground.
3. Breathe together, noticing how the breath moves each of your bodies individually and together. Notice how it feels to have someone supporting you to stretch and be open.
4. Switch roles and notice how it feels to offer this support to your partner.

# Find Your Reasons for Being

Although a sense of purpose is key to a good life, the truth is that many modern pursuits are shallow and bound to leave you feeling empty. The pursuit of wealth and material things often leaves people feeling hollow because it's never-ending. Of course you want to have enough in life and not scrape by. But ultimately hope needs to be anchored in depth. It needs to be based in positive values like service, contribution, and the greater good. If you're lacking a sense of meaning in your life, it might be time to reflect on what it's all for. The concept of *ikigai*, a Japanese term that means "reason for being," may help you find this focus. It's a way of finding something for your life at the intersection of what you're passionate about, what you're called to do, your work, and your mission.

Draw four overlapping circles on a sheet of paper so that they intersect in the middle like a Venn diagram. In one circle, write: "what I am good at." In the next circle, write: "what I love." In the next: "what the world needs." And finally, in the last circle write: "what I can get paid to do." In each circle, write down the things you enjoy in each category. See if you can find things that overlap. For example, maybe you love to bake, the world needs to eat, and you are good at it too. If you can find something that ticks all four boxes, imagine how it would feel to throw all of your being into that pursuit.

# Take Responsibility for What's Yours

If you're someone with a large heart and in a position to help others, you can feel this responsibility like carrying the world on your shoulders. It's a wonderful gift, to care so much and to want to do good in the world. But it can also be overwhelming. You might feel guilty for all that you have and that others do not. After surviving a terrible tragedy, there's a concept called survivor's guilt: People feel guilty for the very fact that they survived and others did not. Unfortunately, self-guilt can be paralyzing instead of motivating. Try this little exercise when you need a bit of perspective to find the balance of what's within your responsibility.

1. Write down everything you feel guilty about by completing the sentence: "I am guilty because…"
2. Take each sentence you wrote down and replace the word "guilty" with "responsible."
3. Read each sentence out loud. How does it read to say you are responsible for these things? Are you *responsible* for poverty? For wars? For climate change? For someone else's death or disease?
4. Release any thoughts of being responsible for creating things that have been out of your control.
5. Reflect on what kind of responsibility you want to take for helping. What is in your ability and capacity to do? Can you make a contribution, no matter how small? This now isn't about alleviating your guilt, but about proactively deciding how you can best be a positive force in the world.

✦

We can easily
forgive a child
who is afraid of
the dark; the real
tragedy of life
is when men are
afraid of the light.

—PLATO
*Greek philosopher*

# Open Your Heart to Hope

When you're closed off and putting up a wall around your heart you might be trying to block out the things that could hurt you to protect yourself. But you'll also be blocking out the good from reaching you. Life requires of you a strong and open heart, willing to be challenged and hurt and to keep beating in your chest full of life anyway. When you need a boost of heart strength, try these gentle yoga backbends that help to stretch across the front of your chest.

1. First, warm up your spine with some gentle Cat/Cow movement. In a tabletop position with your wrists stacked under your shoulders and your knees in line with your hips, move in an intuitive way to alternately arch and round your back. Take several rounds of breath here.
2. Next, take your elbows to where your palms were, pressing your forearms strong into the ground. Lower your forehead and chest toward the ground, arching your spine and shuffling your knees back a bit if you need to in order to find a nice stretch in your back in this puppy shape. Breathe here.
3. Pull yourself forward onto your belly by gripping strong with your palms and forearms and sliding your legs back so that you can raise your head and chest in a sphinx shape.
4. Lastly, pressing back from your arms, come into a Child's Pose by sitting back on your heels, rounding your spine over your thighs and resting in this countermove after those soft back and chest stretches.

# Make Your Younger Self Proud

What did you want to be when you grew up? Children often get asked this question and it's not often that the answer is something that comes true. But it can be fun to think about this and what your younger self wanted for your life. What kind of person did you want to be when you were a kid? What kind of people did you look up to and admire and want to be like? What did you think you would do with your life? When was the last time you thought about these dreams? Where did they go? How do you feel about them now? Even if they haven't come true, are there principles or values within them that you have held to that you're proud of?

Write a letter to yourself from a younger you. Picture yourself in your childhood room, surrounded by all the things you loved at age ten. Reflect on the person you've become. What does your younger self think of you? Notice how writing this makes you feel. Perhaps you are proud of yourself. Perhaps there are ways life has taken you that have fallen out of alignment with what you wanted for yourself. Perhaps you have changed and grown in different ways and what you used to want is no longer reflecting what you want now. Read the letter aloud to yourself and hold both your younger self and your present self with compassion.

# Time-Travel to the End of Your Life

It might seem morbid to think about yourself on your deathbed, but this can be an interesting exercise to focus on the kind of life you hope to lead and how this aligns with what you're doing now. It's a way to potentially prevent regret when you come to look back on your life. Bronnie Ware, a palliative care nurse, wrote a book about the top five regrets of the dying in which she found that there are several common themes when people look back on their lives. They wish they'd been true to themselves and worried less about what others thought. They wish they hadn't worked so much and lived more. They wish they'd expressed their feelings more. They wish they'd kept more in touch with people they care about. And they wish they had made more room to be happy.

Write yourself a letter from yourself at age eighty. Imagine you are looking back on your life. What do you hope it contained? What was good about the life you hope you've lived? Do you have advice for your younger self now? Thinking of the common regrets of people at the end of their lives, is there anything you want to tell your younger self to change or keep doing? Make a plan to review this letter every year to see if you are aligned with what your older self hopes to be able to say about you.

✦

I feel very
adventurous. There
are so many doors
to be opened, and
I'm not afraid to
look behind them.

—ELIZABETH TAYLOR
*English-American actress and humanitarian*

# Have a Non-Zero Day

If you're in the grips of despair and despondency, you could lose all motivation. This is a deep crisis of hope to find your way out of. It can seem like a mountain to climb and starting out on the path up is daunting. Break it down by having a "non-zero" day. This is a day where you take one action, however minuscule, toward your goals and what you want for your life. One of anything is bigger than zero. If your goal is to get fit and healthy, do one push-up or one jumping jack. If you want to write a book, write one page. If you want to get a new job, write one job application. If you're seeking a meaningful relationship, make one new contact. If it's 11:59 and about to strike midnight and you have taken zero actions today, what is the one thing you can do in this minute to say it was not a zero day? As long as it's not zero, your efforts *will* add up over time. There is no way that they can't. You will look behind you one day and realize you're halfway up the mountain because of all the tiny daily steps you've taken.

# Imagine Your Ideal Day

There are seeming contradictions in this book when you really start to live in hope. You need to be open to the wonder of possibility in the future and believe that things could be different or better than they are now. But you also need to live in the present with acceptance or your life will pass you by in dreams for an imagined future that might never arrive. As author Annie Dillard said, how you spend your days is how you spend your life. Try this visualization focused on your ideal average day to build a life of hope in the here and now while also making room for new possibilities.

1. Tell yourself a story of your ideal average day using the present tense. Your usual day might not currently feature all these things you hope for, but tell it to yourself as if it does. Notice what it feels like to be clear on what this ideal average day looks like.

2. Next, tell yourself a story of your ideal day if there were no limits at all. If it were extraordinary, not average. Again, imagine this using the present tense as if you already have this life and notice how this feels to you.

3. Notice the difference between these two visions. Consider one thing from your ideal fantasy day that you could work toward having in some way. Consider what makes up your more realistic average day. Can you approach this with gratitude and self-acceptance for what you do have?

# Make Space for Hope

Physical clutter is stress-inducing, but you might not even realize how the environment you spend most of your time in is affecting your mindset. Think of the unnecessary stuff you accumulate as taking up space and creating mental burdens that get in the way of being satisfied with the simple things. When you're constantly unsatisfied, you are in a grasping state of mind rather than an expansive hopeful state. Try these tips for decreasing the clutter in your home to create a calmer environment.

- Pull the Marie Kondo technique. Go through your things and donate, give away, or toss anything that isn't bringing joy to your life.
- Tidy up by always bringing one thing with you to put away when you go from room to room.
- If you spot a mess or chore and it will take less than five minutes to do, do it as soon as you see it.
- When it comes to consuming and buying more and more things, ask yourself if you can afford it and if you need it. If you feel you do, before you purchase it ask yourself if you'll use it.

There are some four million different kinds of animals and plants in the world. Four million different solutions to the problems of staying alive.

—DAVID ATTENBOROUGH
*English broadcaster and natural historian*

# Take a Forest Bath

No, this isn't about skinny-dipping in a lake. A forest bath is a Japanese practice about spending time in nature, in a wild place far from the concrete jungle cities many live in these days. Connecting to something outside yourself is key to building resilience, and that connection can be found in the beauty of the trees, the open sky, or your feet on the grass. Here are some tips to get the most out of a mindful forest bath.

- Leave your phone at home or in the car. Take this time away from distractions that pull you out of the moment and that get in between the connection you're trying to consciously cultivate in nature.
- Move slowly. Notice the different leaves on the trees. Look up and through the crowns of the trees to the clouds in the sky. Listen to your footsteps and the sounds of the birds and the rustling of the trees in the breeze. Take in the fresh air and scents of the forest. Feel the texture of bark, mushrooms, and flower petals in the undergrowth.
- Breathe deeply. Take the time to consider how the trees around you are like the planet's lungs, cycling fresh air, and you are connected via this process of breathing.
- If your mind wanders from what you're experiencing, try to guide it back to the present by focusing on everything your senses are taking in.

# Breathe Like a Bumblebee

This exercise is another great one for grounding yourself in the present and checking in with your inner world. If you feel bombarded by everything going on around you, it may help to take this little break somewhere quiet so that you can shut out the swirling outside noise for a moment and return to a positive, peaceful place within.

1. Sit somewhere comfortable and relax your body as you start to notice your natural breath.
2. Using your hands, you will symbolically "close" your senses. Place your pinky fingers under your bottom lip and your ring fingers above your top lip to rest under your nose. Your middle fingers will sit under your eyes and your index finger will gently go on top of your closed eyelids. Lastly, your thumb will press softly into the space in front of your ears.
3. Take a deep breath in and as you exhale, hum to yourself with a "bzzzzz."
4. Notice how this feels within you as you close off input from your other senses. You might feel the vibration between your teeth or in your head.
5. Repeat, buzzing with every exhale, for a total of five rounds of breath.
6. Pause to notice how you feel.

◆

For most of us the problem isn't that we aim too high and fail—it's just the opposite—we aim too low and succeed.

—SIR KEN ROBINSON
*English author, speaker, and education advisor*

# Bet On Yourself

Is there something you're trying to do, but are struggling to commit to? Is it difficult to create the habits that will get you where you want to be? Hope is little more than wishful thinking if it's not underpinned by action. But even when you really want something it can be difficult to take the steps you know will be best for you in the long run. If you commit to something with social consequences it can help. It's why having a gym buddy is more likely to get you lacing up your running shoes—you might be tempted on your own to sleep in, but when someone else is relying on you, you'll show up so that you don't let them down. If you have a big goal and need a bit of a social push to achieve it, try publicly announcing it, for example on social media. Just be careful with this, because making an announcement might make you feel like you've taken action when you've actually only been talking about it. This is more about having accountability to drive you forward. Try putting money on it to raise the stakes even higher. Tell a friend what you're trying to do and if you don't do it by a certain date, they can collect. Place a bet on yourself that you can do this.

# Make a Plan; Break It Down

Spend some time in concerted hope by dreaming up your future. Then, actually find actions you can take that will bring you closer to it. This exercise starts with the grand and zooms in to the actionable.

1. Make a list of all the things you want to do in your life before you die. Think about all the experiences you want to have, the places you want to see, the things you want to achieve, the person you want to be. Nothing is too outlandish or impossible for this list. If you had a magic wand, what would you secretly want to do?

2. Write a story about what your ideal life looks like five years from now. Be as specific as you can, but dream big. Life could look very different in five years. Where are you living? Who are you with? What are they like? What are you doing with your days?

3. Write a story about what your life ideally looks like one year from today. Again, be detailed here. Life might not be radically different in one year, but it will be going in the right direction toward your five-year vision. What does that look like?

4. Write out three to five goals you want to accomplish in the next year that will help make that life one year from now a reality.

5. For each goal, write out two or three specific actions you can take toward the goal in the next month.

6. Check in on these goals every month to remind yourself where you're headed and to revise your action steps to keep moving in that direction.

# Figure Out Where Your Time Goes

These days it often feels as though being "busy" is a badge of honor. Have you ever sat back to wonder what exactly you're so busy doing? Being busy is a distraction. It crowds out hope. It enables you to constantly be moving and never sit still long enough to figure out if what you're doing is truly aligned to your purpose. Take a time inventory to find out where you might be out of balance.

1. Write down the activities that you do in a typical day and how many hours you spend doing it each week. Include the time you spend working, socializing, reading, watching TV, scrolling social media, exercising, cooking, eating, on chores, and on hobbies.
2. For each item, rank how much that activity adds to your life on a scale of one to ten with one being it adds nothing and ten being it makes you feel completely satisfied and fulfilled.
3. Review your list. Circle any items on which you are spending a lot of time in a week but your fulfillment score is low. Circle any items where you are spending little time, but your fulfillment score is high.
4. Identify where you might want to make some changes to create more balance between the time you spend on things and what these things add to your life.

✦

# May your choices reflect your hopes, not your fears.

—NELSON MANDELA
*Former president of South Africa*

# Stop Comparing

Comparison is a thief of joy and resentment is an enemy of hope. When you're envying what someone else has, you make yourself small. You prevent hope from working its magic within you because you stifle it. It's like throwing a blanket on a fire and snuffing it out, depriving it of the oxygen it needs to burn. When you compare and feel jealous, you fail to see what you already have and you fail to see the possibilities because your field of vision is taken up with someone else. Bring your focus back to hope by eliminating comparison. Compare yourself only to yourself from yesterday. Make your benchmark your own standards, not someone else's.

Catch your thoughts of resentment and write them down. Empty your mind of these concerns in as much detail as you can. Allow yourself to be as petty as you like while releasing these words from your mind on to the paper. Notice how it makes you feel, to be conscious of these comparisons and how small they make you feel. In a safe place, such as an outdoor fire pit, burn this paper. Watch the flames consume your resentment, ill will, and jealousy like fuel until it turns to ash and all that is left is the light. Check-in again with how you feel, having released these thoughts and feelings.

# Press Wildflowers

Wildflowers are a beautiful symbol of strength and resilience. They seem so delicate, but grow tall, producing colorful blooms that feed bees and other insects, before they scatter their seeds to start the cycle over again, trusting that the wind will carry them where they need to go. Spend some time pressing flowers to serve as a reminder to grow where you are planted.

1. Go for a mindful walk somewhere wildflowers grow.
2. Spend some time watching the flowers and grasses sway in the wind and seeing the insects flitting from bloom to bloom.
3. Select a small handful of flowers to cut and take with you. Choose a few blooms to press that are at their peak brightness and color.
4. Place the flowers you want to press between two sheets of parchment paper and tuck this into a heavy book. You can also place more books or heavy objects on top to compress it further.
5. Leave the flowers alone for about a month. Remove them at this time and check that they are dried out. You can now place them somewhere, such as clipped to your bathroom mirror, on a picture frame on a shelf, or on your fridge, where you'll see them and be reminded of the resilience of seemingly fragile and delicate beautiful things.

# Confront Negative Reinforcement

Have you ever felt you want to be more positive, but for some reason always find yourself reacting and negative? Perhaps it comes out as drama in your life that you know is destructive but you can't seem to help attracting. Perhaps it's in attention-seeking, where you momentarily feel good by acting out and this elicits a response from others. Maybe you guard yourself against anything that feels too good out of the fear that it will disappear if you let yourself have it. If any of this sounds familiar, you could be anchoring yourself in the negative as a place where you're comfortable operating. It's scary to move more into your own power—to claim your hope and live in positive belief, without fear. Sit with yourself for a moment and consider what you're getting out of acting hopeless and helpless. Why is it more comfortable? What are you avoiding thinking about or doing because this is taking all your attention? What would it feel like to release these negative needs, these reinforcers of your negativity? Could you show up as your own best friend and release the need for drama or attention? Believe you deserve to live without this negativity with this mantra: "I create the conditions of positivity for my life."

✦

Lock up your libraries if you like; but there is no gate, no lock, no bolt that you can set upon the freedom of my mind.

—VIRGINIA WOOLF
*English writer*

# Flip Your Perspective Upside Down

The beauty of change and uncertainty, as difficult and painful as it can sometimes be, is that it can help you to realize the potential of hope. You might not have chosen some of the things that happen to you, but there is still power in knowing that things *can* change—that the possibilities are endless. Literally flip your perspective upside down with this Downward Dog yoga shape and consider the opportunities in the unknown.

1. Warm up your spine by standing tall, with your feet hip-distance apart. Place your hands on your hips and hinge forward at the hips into a forward fold.
2. Flow in your spine by inhaling to a flat back, sliding your hands up your shins to the tops of your thighs and shining the crown of your head forward and then exhaling to release and fold forward. Repeat this flowing movement for several rounds of breath.
3. Plant your palms on the floor and step one foot back and then the other so that you are in a plank position with your feet hip-distance apart and your palms stacked straight under your shoulders.
4. Press your hips up and back into Downward Dog. Press your ankles back, but know that it's not the goal to have them touch the ground. Keep your legs strong, engage support from your core and let your head hang heavy as you gaze between your legs.
5. Tune in to your breath as you take in the world upside down for several rounds of breath.
6. When you're ready, lower your knees to the ground and come to sit down and reflect on this new perspective.

# Wonder with Sonder

So much conflict in life comes between people through misunderstanding. As you look out to the world from your own mind and eyes alone, you inevitably see things from your perspective. You might feel as though others don't understand or don't care. This can be profoundly isolating, leading to feelings of hopelessness and powerlessness. Approach others in your life with compassion. Assume first that most people are good at heart and trying their best, even when it doesn't look like it to you or it comes into conflict with your good heart and your good efforts. The concept of "sonder" is helpful to remember in these moments. Sonder refers to the realization that everyone—including the stranger who served you coffee this morning, the person across from you on the bus, the coworker who always seems annoyed with you—has an inner world and experience that is as complex and wonderful as yours and of which you only know a fraction (as they, too, only know a fraction of your inner being). Feel connected in this pause of remembering that you don't have the full story of what someone else is going through. You never can fully know. But you can be open and vulnerable in this recognition of the mutual condition of unknowing that you both share.

# Remember the Goal

There is no arrival point when it comes to personal development. It sounds disheartening as you work so hard on living in hope, but you will never arrive at a perfect state of being. Because hope is forward-facing, when you do succeed in realizing your hopes, you leave them behind. You have what you long sought in the present, so what do you hope for now? Author Mark Manson argues that in this sense, hope is, in essence, a necessarily destructive force. Hope requires an ongoing conflict with the present moment and what you are experiencing now. This doesn't have to be a hopeless realization, however. It might be that hope requires you to believe and to take action *while* cultivating love in the present. This is where the goal of mindfulness comes in. Your practice isn't about the time you spend sitting in meditation or the time you spend journaling about your hopes or visualizing your future. It's about how these practices bring you greater peace and less reactivity in the present so that you can enjoy your life in the moment while still feeling purposeful for your future. This won't be an epiphany of enlightenment. This is your life's work: the work of becoming.

◆

Nothing in life is to be feared, it is only to be understood. Now is the time to understand more, so that we may fear less.

—MARIE CURIE
*French-Polish physicist*

# Surrender with Grace

Letting go of what's not meant for you can be easier said than done when it's something you really want and you have a fixed idea of what it looks like. It's still a necessary process to go through to make room for what *is* for you. You can't build a healthy relationship when you're stuck in one where you're begging for crumbs. You won't find your dream job when you're making decisions out of fear. You won't be moving toward all that you can have in life when you're clinging to something that has limits you can't control. At these times, you need to surrender to the process of becoming who you are meant to be. Surrender doesn't mean giving up. It's about accepting what you need to in order to move on when otherwise you will remain stuck. It doesn't mean you need to like it. It doesn't mean you shouldn't take action and pursue what you want or change things that aren't working. But it means trusting that what is meant for you will come. When you're encountering resistance external to you, it might be time to give in to it rather than fight it. Try this affirmation at these times: "I surrender with grace."

# Let Go of Whatever Holds You Back

Building an optimistic mindset is only half of the equation. If you don't tackle any negative thoughts, patterns, and beliefs, you won't feel much different. A great way to practice letting go is to start with your body. Come to this body scan meditation to release physical tension you hold on to and to work on letting go of whatever no longer serves you.

1. Lie down in a comfortable position.
2. Take your attention to your feet and slowly move your focus up your entire body, taking note of any areas of sensation—tightness, tingling, tension, holding on, resisting.
3. Next, beginning at your feet again, inhale and tense your toes, feet, and ankles as hard as you can.
4. Exhale and let everything go.
5. Keep moving slowly up your body, tensing with an inhale and relaxing with an exhale. Clench your calves, knees, and thighs. Squeeze your bum and abs. Make fists and bring tension into your arms, shoulders, and upper back. Close your jaw, shut your eyes, and furrow your brow.
6. Scan your full body again, noticing if any particular areas of tension you felt from the start are still there or if you've been able to let them go through this exercise of purposely creating resistance and relaxing it. Release any fear, anxiety, or hopelessness that might correspond with the physical tightness you hold.

✦

# Rules for happiness: something to do, someone to love, something to hope for.

—IMMANUEL KANT
*German philosopher*

# Write Down Your Hopes

Make hope a less abstract feeling by writing down what you want for yourself in different areas of your life. On a piece of paper, write down four headings: Health, Relationships, Work, and Leisure. Write down at least five things you desire in your life in each category by starting with "I want…." You can include things you already have achieved or have in your life because it might be that you are very satisfied in some aspects of your life already. But try to dream big here.

Once you have your list, on a new sheet of paper recreate it but for each item you wrote down get more specific. This can help you to really hone in on not only what you want, but how it will look. For example, you might have written that you want to get fit under your health category. Get more specific by asking yourself how much weight you want to lose in the next three months or how you plan to do it or why. Using the same example, you might write that you want to be able to go for a walk every day or climb the stairs without getting out of breath or be able to lift your niece onto your shoulders. If your first draft still isn't specific enough, do this again to get to a level of detail that feels more actionable. Looking at your list you should be able to see where you can get started toward these dreams sooner rather than later.

# Create Synchronicity

Sometimes in life things happen that you can't quite explain. It feels like more than a coincidence and suddenly you're seeing signs everywhere. Synchronicity can make you feel like the stars are aligning. You're more attuned to seeing opportunities when they present themselves. You can create this in your life by getting clear on what you want and simply paying attention. Try this exercise to see for yourself.

1. Write down the top thing you desire in your life that you don't currently have.
2. Over the course of the next month, watch out for any sign taking you toward this dream or goal. These could be very small. It might be crossing paths with someone who can help you. It might be seeing an advertisement for a course or an opportunity that would nudge you in this new direction. It might be a repeating phrase, symbol, or color that reminds you of your dreams for yourself and inspires hope in you.
3. Take a photo of everything you notice and save it into a central file or print it out and tack it to a board.
4. At the end of the month, review your photos and notice if you're more attuned to the synchronicity around you that is taking you toward your dream.

# Bake a Delicious Treat

Hope doesn't require fancy, large plans. You can find hope in the smallest of ways by coming back to what truly matters. Nourish yourself and others by baking a treat. If you have an old family recipe you haven't made in a while, find the old card, and roll up your sleeves. Feel connected to the wisdom and knowledge of your ancestors in the present moment as you create something that provides sustenance and pleasure. Slow down to create something better than what you could buy off the shelf. Notice how the ingredients come together to form something that is greater than the sum of their parts. Mindfully take in the scent of this recipe filling your home and taking you back to memories of your parents or grandparents using these same ingredients and dressing their table with the same food you are preparing. Share what you've made with someone and let it bring you together over your mutual enjoyment of this treat.

◆

Everyone has oceans to fly, if they have the heart to do it. Is it reckless? Maybe. But what do dreams know of boundaries?

—AMELIA EARHART
*American aviator*

# Move to Get Unstuck

Sometimes it can feel like, despite the work you're doing on yourself and your hopeful mindset, things just aren't moving. You might feel stuck and as if things will never change. Bear in mind that this is often an intense feeling that you will go through right before you level up. You are breaking through old patterns, habits, and ways of believing. It can feel like you're being held down when you're about to break through to the other side. When you need to feel things starting to move, try this flowing sun breath meditation.

1. Sitting either in a chair with no armrests or on the floor cross-legged, find length throughout your spine as you sit tall.
2. Take a deep breath, in and out through your nose.
3. On your next big inhale, sweep your arms out to the side and up overhead like you're carving a rainbow over yourself. Keep your shoulders away from your ears as you do.
4. Exhale, lowering your arms out to the side and down to rest again beside you.
5. Repeat for at least five cycles of breath, seeing if you can touch your fingers at the top of your inhale just as you finish taking in your breath, and grazing the floor or your chair just as you complete your exhale. Move and breathe slowly.
6. Pause to notice how you feel and whether this sense of moving energy can carry you into the rest of your day.

# Dismantle Resistance

There's a saying about love that goes back to the poet Rumi: It isn't your job to go out trying to find love, but to look within yourself to dismantle all of the barriers within you that block it from you. Love is an infinite resource that is all around, not something you need to hunt out. You just can't see it until you work on yourself and what makes you blind to it. And so, too, with hope. The language of hope is often similar—that it's necessary to "find" hope. You grope for it when facing despair and helplessness, like it's a life raft at sea. What's needed is actually to find the barriers within you that resist it. Hope is equally infinite and everywhere. Search not for hope, but for the assumptions that limit you. What beliefs hold you back? Do you feel deserving? Do you feel others understand? Do you feel someone will help? Wherever you feel a hint of internal resistance to what you truly want for yourself, focus here. Investigate it with honesty and openness. Tear down the walls that keep you from hope and you will find it waiting for you there on the shore all along.

✦

And now here is my secret, a very simple secret: It is only with the heart that one can see rightly; what is essential is invisible to the eye.

—ANTOINE DE SAINT-EXUPÉRY
*French writer*

# Hold Hands

Have you ever been nervous about something and then calmed by the simple touch of another person? A pat on the back when you're going in to a test. Someone reaching out from beside a hospital bed. A head on a shoulder after a long day. When you need a boost of hope, find someone to sit with and hold their hand. Studies have found that the simple act of holding hands reduces stress. If you hold hands with someone close to you, the effect is even greater. When you cuddle up with someone, your feel-good hormones like oxytocin are produced. It's another reminder of how connected the mind and body are. You can't always rationalize away your swirling thoughts when things are tough. But you can calm your body through these simple ways of physically connecting to someone in your life. It's also a beautiful gift to give to someone else who is struggling. Sometimes it's not always clear how to help someone and you can feel helpless yourself as a result. Give this gift of touch and you'll create a mutual exchange of hopeful energy that grows as it passes between you.

# Fall In Love with Everything

Hope can lead you to live in an imagined future and cost you the experience of what is good in your life in the present moment. Don't get locked into thinking you can't be happy until what you hope for comes true. A deeper sense of lasting hope can be found in acceptance. It's part of what makes the difference between someone who is defeated by adversity and someone who is developed through it—accepting both the good and bad things that happen to you and finding meaning in these experiences. One way to practice this is to radically love everything that happens. A sad situation is still going to make you feel sad. But allow room within you for all of life's richness of experience with this meditation.

1. Sit in a comfortable position with some back support.
2. Start to notice how you feel and your breath, inhaling and exhaling through your nose.
3. As thoughts arise, acknowledge them with love. You could even visualize embracing the thought into a tight hug. You might be worried or anxious. Love that you don't know what's going to happen. You might be struggling with painful feelings. Love that you have a deep well of caring within you. You might feel hopeless about a situation. Love that you are being challenged to grow.
4. At the end of your meditation, notice how you feel. Is there any new lightness to the shape of your thoughts as you practice radically loving everything about them?

# Write New Rules

To live in hope might mean tossing out the old rules you used to live by. Out with the negative, in with the positive. It might take time to embed this into your daily way of being. Write at least five rules for hope that you will live by. Draw your rules out on some pretty colored paper and stick them somewhere you will see them and be reminded of your commitment to yourself, such as your fridge, your bathroom mirror, or at your desk. Your rules will be unique to you, but here are some you might draw inspiration from.

In order to live in hope, I must:

- Surround myself with hopeful people.
- Trust that I can influence the course of my life.
- Find meaning and learn from all my experiences—the good and the not-so-good.
- Take care of my mind and body.
- Believe in infinite possibilities.

✦

Do your little bit
of good where
you are; it's those
little bits of good
put together that
overwhelm the
world.

—DESMOND TUTU
*South African theologian and human rights activist*

# Channel Pain Into a Cause

Witnessing the injustice of the world can make you angry. Anger is a tough emotion to handle. It can consume you. But it also shows the depth of your feeling. It is evidence that you hope for something better, not just for yourself, but for others. So you have a choice with how you handle this anger. You can become embittered that things aren't as you want them to be. You can protest them from a helpless place, beating your fists against a solid concrete wall. Or, you can choose to channel your anger into a cause. You can become accountable for your role. You can rise up from a hopeful place, beating a drum that others might follow. You can be an example, living from your authentic truth.

This could look different depending on your gifts and how you choose to show up. Join a cause you are passionate about and volunteer where you're needed. Publish words that you stand by to generate awareness. Donate to a fund doing good. Learn more about the problem. Add your voice to a crowd at a protest. Write to your elected representatives. Ask a neighbor if you can help with anything. Do your little bit of good in whatever way you can. As the saying goes, small drops of water make a mighty ocean.

# Shape Your Future in the Present

You are the sum of your past thoughts and actions. Where you are as you read this book is a direct result of your choices and beliefs from the past. This isn't to say that everything that has happened to you has been of your choosing. Remember, much of life is not in your control. At the same time, you do have influence over how you choose to respond to what happens to you and this is based in your own will. You have more control over your own thoughts and how you see things than you think. If you're hoping for a better future, spend some time thinking about how the ways you think and act have brought you to where you are now. Then, ask yourself if your thoughts and actions in the present are taking you on a track to your desires or if they're unchanged from the past. To see your future, look at your present thoughts and actions. Where are these taking you?

# Index

Affirmations, 5, 9, 157, 237. *See also* Mantras

Alter ego, 33

Baking/cooking activities, 66, 168, 211, 242

Balance, finding, 119, 129, 227

Battle plans, 172

Best-case scenarios, 56–57

Body awareness, 41–42, 45, 62, 94, 149, 207, 238

Body scan meditation, 42, 62, 149, 238

Boundaries, 116, 170, 243

Breathing techniques, 25, 44, 74, 88, 133, 162, 223, 244. *See also* Meditations

Bucket list, 65

Calm, finding, 25, 44, 52–54, 111, 133, 149, 162, 168, 195, 220. *See also* Peace

Candles, lighting, 6, 41

Catastrophes, 4, 56–57, 128

Causes, helping with, 73, 130, 251

Changes, accepting, 16, 147, 150, 187

Changes, making, 96, 102, 163, 233

Chants, 81, 107

Character, building, 144

Chatter, reducing, 33, 82

Child-self, 68–69, 166, 215

Choices, making, 75, 173, 228, 252

Clutter, eliminating, 220

Comparisons, 100, 198–99, 229

Compassion, 40, 139, 153, 177, 215, 234

Compliment list, 110

Control, focus on, 50, 58, 101, 135, 200, 252

Control, loss of, 13, 148, 156

Control, releasing, 48, 114, 194, 212, 237

Creative activities, 32, 60, 66, 137, 164, 166, 169

Dancing, 117

Date with self, 158

Death, reflecting on, 11, 216

Despair, countering, 57, 62, 76, 108, 119, 181, 218

Disappointment, handling, 32, 59, 93, 104, 119, 134, 198

Dislikes, eliminating, 185

Distractions, reducing, 70, 156, 158, 189–90, 222–23, 227

Dressing up, 197

Electronic devices, 70, 189–90

Emotions, freeing, 111, 181

Emotions, observing, 7, 30, 53, 156

Emotions, sharing, 175–76, 184, 246

Empowerment, 18, 48, 100

Enough, having, 131, 211

Fear, overcoming, 209, 236

Fixing things, 84, 128, 150

Flow, going with, 119

Flowers, 24, 64, 168, 222, 230

Forest bath, 195, 222

Forgiveness, 21, 61, 203, 213

Future, dreams of, 69, 118, 137, 152, 160, 172–73, 179, 186, 226, 235, 252

Future, possibilities for, 11, 31, 38, 56–58, 65, 69, 91–92, 118, 219

Gardens, planting, 86, 130, 230

Gifts, cherishing, 73

Goals, achieving, 159–60, 171–72, 218, 224–26, 235

Goals, listing, 65, 226

God/goddess, 94

Gratitude, 34, 125, 127, 178, 203

Grief, 15, 150, 181

Grounding techniques, 13, 25, 57, 223

Growth, post-traumatic, 89, 145

Growth mindset, 77, 89, 103, 144–45

Habits, breaking, 244

Habits, creating, 18, 225

Hands, holding, 247

Happiness, noting, 85, 124

Happiness, rules for, 239

Harm, doing no, 148

Health, caring for, 196, 240

Helping others, 38, 49, 188, 193, 205, 212, 247, 250

Helplessness, shifting, 19, 57, 101–2, 231, 245, 251

Hero's Journey, 38

Highlights/lowlights, 29

Hope, box of, 142

Hope, color of, 143

Hope, dreams of, 69, 105, 118. *See also* Future

Hope, haven of, 80

Hope, jar of, 186

Hope, maintaining, 18, 24, 35, 55, 58–59, 95, 120, 173

Hope, opening heart to, 214

Hopelessness, shifting, 14, 76, 104, 192, 231, 234, 238

Hopes, listing, 65, 226, 240

Ideal day/life, 118, 219, 226

Impermanence, 23, 53, 104, 150

Inspiration, 141, 174, 186, 218, 241, 249. *See also* Motivations

Journal activities, 18, 29, 34, 58, 82, 85, 106, 184, 193, 199, 235. *See also* Writing exercises

Laughter, 37

Letters, writing, 92, 127, 157, 161, 215–16

Letting go, 17, 28, 38, 185, 199, 203, 237–38

Life, as movie, 151

Life, beauty of, 20, 63–64, 67, 136

Light, power of, 6, 41, 108–9, 132, 135, 213

Limits, eliminating, 69, 71–72, 79, 103

Love, embracing, 39, 248

Love meditation, 177, 248

Luck, finding, 26, 60

Mantras, 21–23, 46, 80, 89, 110, 122, 125, 131, 146, 150, 231. *See also* Affirmations

Meditation, body scan, 42, 62, 149, 238

Meditation, gratitude, 125

Meditation, laughter, 37

Meditation, love, 177, 248

Meditation, mindful, 14, 96, 126, 148. *See also* Mindful exercises

Meditation, moving, 117, 244

Meditation, with partner, 182

Meditation techniques, 40, 62, 104, 112, 117, 119, 131, 201, 235

Mentors, 38, 165

Mindful exercises, 27, 41–42, 62, 82, 195, 207, 230, 242

Mindful meditation, 14, 96, 126, 148. *See also* Meditations

Mindset, choosing, 77, 160, 232, 238, 244

Mindset, of growth, 77, 89, 103, 144–45

Mission statement, 9

Moon, howling at, 123

Moon, rising of, 132

Motivations, 9, 11, 76, 165, 190–91, 218. *See also* Inspiration

Moving forward, 21, 58, 78, 89, 134, 167, 183, 237–38, 244

Moving meditation, 117, 244

Nature, appreciating, 20, 64, 68, 195, 222, 230

Negative feelings, 7, 104, 125, 154, 175–76, 180, 183, 189, 231

Negative thoughts, 26–27, 29, 60, 82, 110, 115, 122, 139, 177, 231, 238

New chapter, opening, 152

New rules, writing, 249

New skills, learning, 97

Noise, reducing, 189, 223

Obstacles, overcoming, 46, 56–57, 89, 152, 172, 200

Optimism, 5, 36–37, 78, 94, 96, 103, 129, 133, 138, 180, 238. *See also* Positive thinking

Partner, meditating with, 182

Past, reflecting on, 58, 134, 203, 215–16, 252

Pauses, 12–13, 17

Peace, finding, 40, 62, 85, 135, 158, 168, 177, 223, 235. *See also* Calm

Perfectionism, 146, 200

Perspectives, changing, 68, 102–3, 113, 150, 233–34

Pessimism, 96, 103, 139, 142, 154. *See also* Negative thoughts

Pets, caring for, 208

Physical activities, 48, 98, 148, 160, 166, 210, 218

Play, time for, 68, 166, 169

Poems, writing, 161

Positive thinking, 9–11, 29, 60, 75, 90, 102, 122, 138–39. *See also* Optimism

Post-traumatic growth, 89, 145

Present, living in, 13, 62, 219, 223, 248, 252

Problems, solving, 97, 106, 221

Professional help, 196

Purpose, embracing, 89, 185, 193, 207, 211, 227

Regrets, 134, 153, 216

Rejection, handling, 180

Relationships, improving, 174, 182, 204–5

Resilience, 14, 17, 21–23, 42–45, 50, 86, 101–3, 164–65, 193, 207, 222, 230

Resistance, 150, 237–38, 245

Responsibility, accepting, 202–3, 212

Rewards, intermittent, 115

Risks, taking, 99, 146, 182, 194, 209–10, 217, 243

Rock bottom, 38, 56, 89, 152

Routines, daily, 18, 29, 82, 136, 155, 206–7, 218

Sacred places, 141

Scents, pleasant, 6, 168, 242

Sculpture, creating, 164

Security, 149

Seeds, planting, 86, 130, 230

Self-care, 49–50, 196–97, 240

Self-compassion, 139, 215

Self-confidence, 33, 57, 78, 100, 197

Self-doubt, 33, 46, 121–22, 131, 172

Self-love, 36, 78, 157

Self-massage, 52

Self-portrait, 100

Self-worth, 36, 49, 78, 110, 139, 157, 170, 180

Setbacks, handling, 180

Solitude, 81, 158, 176, 192, 205

"Sonder" concept, 234

Songs/music, 81, 117

Spiritual beliefs, 141, 193

Spontaneity, 76, 147

Standards, meeting, 100, 198–99, 229

Story, telling, 50, 139, 153, 161

Strengths, embracing, 22, 46–47, 51, 94

Success, 87, 140, 172, 224–25, 235

Support, building, 188, 210

Synchronicity, 241

Taking stock, 9, 22

Time, for play, 68–69, 166

Time, importance of, 11, 216, 227

Trees, climbing, 68

Trust, embracing, 46, 122, 131

Uncertainty, managing, 114, 131, 233

Values, retaining, 154, 199, 211, 215

Vision board, 137

Walks, 68, 230, 240

Warrior Two stance, 48

Willpower, 150, 156, 159

Wishes, extending, 178

Worst-case scenarios, 56–57, 172

Writing exercises, 82, 92, 127, 157, 161, 215–16, 240, 249. *See also* Journal activities

Yoga, 42, 48, 54, 94, 112, 129, 148, 210, 214, 233

# About the Author

Carley Centen is a writer and yoga teacher who first encountered mindfulness as part of her own quest to tackle her general anxiety. Through online courses, in-person retreats, and storytelling, she now draws on over a decade of practice in her mission to share, grow, and continually learn about the ideas and tools that work to improve our bodies, minds, and lives. Carley has taught yoga and mindfulness in places around the world from Costa Rica to Colombia to London.